GOING PLACES

Lake Crescent Lodge

GOING PLACES

Family Getaways in the Pacific Northwest

*by John Bigelow and
Breck Longstreth*

*Seattle's Child Publishing
Seattle, Washington*

LC Card Number: 85-50342

ISBN: 0-9614626-0-4

Introductory material by David Messerschmidt

Design and Production
  Consulting Designer: Ellen Ziegler
  Design: Sonia Cole, Jennifer Summers
  Production: Dona McAdam

Illustrations by Jennifer Summers

Cover photos by Michael Ziegler

Typesetting: Telecom Type by Data and Staff

Thanks to the following:
Gail Barham, Ann & Abe Bergman, Teresa Bigelow & Bill Robertson, Rosalie Bookston, Sandy Clarren, Ellen Cole & Michael Daum, Bob & Sonia Cole, Amy Corey, Debby Cromwell, Carol Ege, Emily Elliott, Ruth Engelberg, Susan Fort, Jeni James, Jerry Keating, Debby Kearnes, Ann Kemp, Linda Kohnstamm, Carolyn Margon, Sally Marks, Laurie Martinelli, Bobbi Martinsen, Marianne Matsumoto, Patti McKillop, David Messerschmidt, Cori Kirkpatrick, Diane Norris, Holly Overman, Dorthy Perlman, Carita Polin, Gail Ranson, Rosemary Rice, Betty Ruddy, Karen Schmidt, Gretchen Shively, Jennifer Summers, Peggy Stamm, Kris Sullivan, Joyce Tomlinson, Roberta Wilkes.

Introduction

Why we needed this book.

We're parents and we enjoy getaways with our kids. We like adventure, but we like to know what we're in for when we all pile into the car. We wanted information about inns, resorts, dude ranches, cabins, motels, hotels—the whole range of Northwest getaway possibilities—that welcomed families. We wanted specific information about what was available, what it cost and how long it would take to get there.

We've relied on other guide books—some are excellent—but they didn't have the detailed information that we wanted to help us plan getaways.

Who we are.

We're Seattle area parents. Six years ago we began publishing a monthly newspaper *Seattle's Child*. What began as another project hatched in the kitchen has become a monthly guide for parents and a comprehensive calendar of children's activities with a circulation of nearly 7000.

Our perspective on family getaways is very personal, we have children and we want to provide ourselves and other parents with reliable information that they won't find in one place anywhere else. We've created quite a list of places to visit. It's long enough that we'll have to save some getaways for visits with our grandchildren.

How we wrote this book.

We started asking family friends and *Seattle's Child* readers to tell us about their favorite family getaways. We wanted secluded spots where we could leave our busy lives behind; as well as a choice of places packed with activities to fill our days with something different. We expanded our inquiry to friends of friends and began to keep a list of all the places mentioned. Once we compiled the list of first choices, we organized them by location in Washington, Oregon, Idaho and British Columbia.

We asked recent getaway visitors to complete a detailed six-page questionnaire. If there were no recent visitors, we offered families a stipend to try out a place and complete our questionnaire. With all that information we selected 59 locations to feature in this edition of *Going Places*.

We contacted the getaways we chose for information on rates and facilities. Our listings were current at press time, but you should always confirm them when you call for reservations.

How to use this book

Browse the table of contents and the quick reference index. We organized information by regions. In each section we include an introduction, information on routes, and "What to see on the way." We also list driving times from Seattle and Portland.

You'll want to supplement the information here with a good map. If you're traveling across the mountain passes during the winter, check weather conditions before you leave and carry chains.

Driving times.

What used to be a reasonable drive before children is often more than we can handle now. A car full of gear, carseats and the family pet can be a party on wheels—or no fun at all. We urge you to temper your plans with the time available for your stay. Save the distant outings for times when you can really enjoy them.

Making reservations.

The surest way to get lodging is to phone for reservations. Many of these places are extremely popular, and some families visit year after year—placing their next year's reservation a year in advance.

Most of these places will accept phone reservations and hold the dates you want pending arrival of a deposit. When you're on the phone make sure they will send written confirmation once they receive your deposit.

School holiday periods are the most heavily booked, but there are last minute cancellations. It won't hurt to make a call and see if there are any openings.

Questions to ask when you make reservations.

What should we bring? What do they supply? Are there well-stocked stores nearby? Also check out the eating arrangements. Ask about bedding. You might save money if you bring your own linens or sleeping bags. Confirm check-in and check-out times. And ask about high chairs, and booster seats and cribs.

Describe your family.

This is a select list. We wanted places that welcomed families. But go ahead and describe your family. If you want to arrange babysitting, do it in advance. That way you can confirm that someone is available and arrange to meet them when you arrive before they actually take on responsibility for watching your children.

Everything changes.

Prices, owners, facilities—we expect them to change. Use us as a guide, but check out the facilities with a phone call or letter to confirm that it will work for your family.

Share your experience.

If you know of other places that we should include in future editions of *Going Places*, or if you have comments about one of the getaways listed please write to us. We want to share as much first hand information as possible.

Going Places
c/o Seattle's Child
P.O. Box 22578
Seattle, WA 98122

Contents

Central & Eastern Washington

Idaho

Oregon

BRITISH
COLUMBIA

Traveling in Canada

Visiting a foreign country is always a special experience. Going to an English-speaking country is not as markedly different as visiting a nation with another language, but there are compensations. You can move around easily, use local means of transportation and get the most out of attractions. And you can communicate with the natives. Official signs and postings in both French and English may look strange in British Columbia, where the French-speaking population is very small compared with Quebec. But this national policy does spark an interest in children. It helps, along with the unfamiliar faces on coins, to impress upon them that Canada is indeed a different country. British Columbia is a huge province, larger than Washington, Oregon and California combined. Most of the population is concentrated in the Vancouver-Victoria area.

A passport is not required of U.S. citizens. U.S. citizens returning after 48 hours can take back $400 (U.S.) worth of merchandise duty free including 32 ounces of alcohol. For visits of less that 48 hours, $25 is allowed. There is virtually no restriction on vehicle entry into Canada. All vehicles should carry a motor vehicle registration form and proof of insurance. Service stations sell regular and unleaded gasoline and many have diesel fuel, particularly along main highways. Driving is on the right side. Right turns are permitted at red lights after stopping. British Columbia law requires the use of seat belts. The exchange of U.S. money into Canadian currency is in favor of the U.S. at this time. Banks generally give the best exchange rate. Businesses displaying a Fair Exchange decal on the window have pledged to exchange dollars at the current bank rate. It is a good idea to use up all your Canadian money before returning. Most U.S. businesses no longer accept Canadian coins, and paper currency has to be exchanged at a bank.

British Columbia does a great job of informing and pleasing visitors. The Tourism B.C. office in Seattle (720 Olive Way, 98101, (206)623-5937) has excellent materials. If you drive and use the

Blaine-Douglas border crossing on I-5, you'll see the Tourism B.C. office on the highway not far north of the border. In Vancouver, the office is downtown at Robson Square.

Although a passport is not required when a U.S. citizen enters Canada, it is a good idea to have a Washington State driver's license with photograph to establish identity. Usually the stop at the border is brief simply to establish home address and citizenship. Inspection of auto trunks for contraband is on a selective basis by both the Canadian and U.S. officers. Persons under 18 traveling without parent or another adult should carry a letter from parent or guardian authorizing them to travel to Canada.

There are duty-free stores on this side of the border where you can purchase liquor, cigarettes and merchandise at advantageous prices as you enter Canada. If you still have these purchases when you recross the border on your way home you must consider them as part of your allowable imports and pay duty if you are over the duty-free limit. There is also a Canadian duty-free store at the Blaine border crossing. Purchases are subject to U.S. customs exemptions and restrictions.

If you want to take a pet dog or cat into Canada you must have a certificate signed by a veterinarian that describes the animal and states that it has been vaccinated against rabies within the past 36 months.

The Royal Canadian Mounted Police are frequently asked to locate people on vacation to give them urgent family messages. The news media, all travel information centers and most campgrounds cooperate in the Tourist Alert Program. Names of persons sought are posted on bright pink Tourist Alert signs.

Reminder: Canada uses the metric system of weights and measures. Converting metric signs into inches, feet, miles and pounds is a good family game. Here are some common conversions: inch equals 2.5 centimeters; foot equals 0.3 meters; mile equals 1.6 kilometers; pound equals 0.45 kilograms.

Vancouver

As gateway to the Pacific and the Orient, Vancouver has a distinctive cosmopolitan flavor. Not only does it have a large and colorful Chinatown, second only in size to San Francisco's, it also has a Little Italy, a Little Japan, and large ethnic groups from India, the Philippines, eastern Europe and southeast Asia. About 40 percent of the school children are from homes where English is not the primary language. People with British ancestry—English, Scottish and Irish—predominate and give the area their flavor.

Only 150 miles and three hours driving time from Seattle, Vancouver has lots of water for sailing and fishing, excellent skiing not far away, and colorful attractions in markets, museums and parks that are appealing to all ages.

Vancouver's 1000-acre Stanley Park is a marvelous combination of waterfront, zoo, aquarium, children's train and playgrounds, walking trails, cycling paths and sports areas. Granville Island, close to downtown, is Seattle's Pike Place Market and Pioneer Square combined. Boats and canoes can be rented near the market and a 12-seat ferry putt-putts from a dock at the Aquatic Centre on English Bay in downtown Vancouver to various stops including the Maritime Museum, False Creek and Granville. At the foot of Granville Street the Sea Bus, part of the city bus system, leaves for North Vancouver. This is a nice little boat trip, but you probably will want at some time to drive across Lion's Gate Bridge to "North Van" where the mountains begin. The Grouse Mountain skyride is an aerial tram that goes up 3700 feet to offer a spectacular view of the Vancouver area. There are ski runs in winter and trails in summer, restaurants and gift shops.

You need not worry about running into rainy weather. The downtown Vancouver area has a wealth of indoor attractions. The Vancouver Museum, Planetarium and Maritime Museum are clustered just west of Granville Island. The Vancouver Art Gallery is downtown just off Robson Street. Its gallery for children with art works hung at their eye level is typical of the gallery's ambience. Robson Street is an area of small European shops, an ice skating rink (your own skates), clothes boutiques, tea rooms, delicatessens and bookstores located in low-rise buildings in the heart of downtown, a tribute to the people's determination to retain an island of grace and style in the midst of high-rise growth.

Gastown is "old Vancouver," east of downtown. It is very touristy and lots of relaxed fun. The University of British Columbia's Anthropology Museum is noted for its totem poles and other Northwest Indian artifacts.

An out of the ordinary six-hour land-sea trip is available from mid-May to September. The Royal Hudson Steam Train leaves from North Vancouver and travels to Squamish. The new excursion ship M.V. Brittania makes the same trip by water. You ride one way by train and the other by boat.

You will be aware that something big is being cooked up for Vancouver. It is Expo 86, a world festival with the theme "Man in Motion." Canadians know how to put on successful expositions. This one will be a dandy, with everything from samples of Halley's Comet, which has returned to the vicinity of earth for the first time in 75 years, to the possibility of landing one of the U.S. space shuttles.

HOW TO GET THERE

Most visitors bound for Vancouver and Whistler take I-5 north and cross the border at Blaine. In British Columbia I-5 becomes Highway 99. There are 13 border crossings for vehicles on the Washington-British Columbia line, but some are not open at all hours. Blaine never closes. Seattle to Vancouver is about 150 miles and three hours driving time.

WHAT TO SEE ON THE WAY

If you are driving to Vancouver or Whistler, please refer to suggestions in the Birch Bay section of this book.

Blue Horizon
Town and Country Inn

1225 Robson St., Vancouver, BC V6E 1C3
1-800-663-1333
Moderate—$40-$100 (Canadian)
CB, MC, V

Directions: Take I-5 north to the U.S.-Canadian border. In Canada, Route 99 goes directly into downtown Vancouver via the Granville Bridge. Stay on Granville to Nelson. Turn left on Nelson west to Burrard. Turn right on Burrard, go north to Robson. Turn left on Robson and drive ½ mile.

At A Glance: Cribs; Kitchens ($7 for operational stove); TV; Restaurant; Indoor pool; Sauna; Hot tub; Babysitting (by pre-arrangement)

All the rooms in this highrise are on corners and have great views and balconies. However, windows open without screens, so adventurous kids should be watched. The Blue Horizon is a comfortable, family-oriented hotel. The service is good, but you feel comfortable carrying your own bags and bringing in groceries. The rooms are large but not fancy. An indoor pool (often highly chlorinated) and sauna are in the basement of the hotel.

Some of the units are equipped with kitchens, but there's an extra $7 fee to get your stove operational. The 32nd floor of the hotel has a restaurant that offers a sumptuous Sunday brunch ($10 adults, $4 kids—Canadian). The view is marvelous and children can spend their time finding places from "up high" they've visited during the day. There's also a coffee shop on the main floor of the hotel. About three blocks away, on Robson, and also in Robson Plaza opposite the skating rink are branches of the restaurant Mozart Konditorei which serves good sandwiches and pastries. Service is rapid except at peak times, high chairs are available, and the front part of the restaurant is a bakery and candy shop. Kids can go and select dessert while they're waiting for the main course.

Comments
"This has a lived-in feeling. It's not too fancy, so that when your kids spill you don't feel too bad."

The Denman Hotel

1733 Comox St., Vancouver, BC V6G 1P6
1-800-663-9494 or 604-688-7711
Expensive—$100-$130 (Canadian); $15 per extra person; children un-
der 18 free in parents' room; various "package deals"
AE, CB, DC, MC, V

At A Glance: Cribs; Kitchens ($10 for operational stove); TV;
Restaurant; Indoor pool; Sauna; Squash and racquetball courts;
Babysitting (by pre-arrangement)

Each of the Denman's 300 guest rooms and suites has a balcony
and a view of the city, mountains or English Bay. All rooms have a
refrigerator and coffee maker, and lots have fully equipped kitchens if
you want to do your own cooking. Rooms are comfortable and very
large—big enough to place a crib unobtrusively in the hallway and spacious enough for a family of four or five.

In addition to the pool and sauna, the Denman has interesting shops
and a supermarket within the building. There's a movie theatre next
door, Stanley Park and the beach at English Bay are a short walk
away, and it's just minutes to the rest of downtown Vancouver. The
hotel is located on a busy, urban street that is active throughout the
day.

There are approximately twenty restaurants located within walking
distance of the Denman, including a McDonald's. The Denman's own
Humphrey's, located on top of the hotel, is geared to adults but has a
nice brunch on Sundays ($10 adults, $6 kids—Canadian).

Comments

"Despite the rain, we have enjoyed the Denman Hotel in the
winter because the accommodations are so self-contained and central
to downtown."

"Because of the size of the rooms, one possibility is to bring along
a teenage babysitter."

"The refrigerator within the suite is a real bonus. Children can eat
breakfast in the room, watch TV and let their parents have time
alone."

The Greenbriar Apts.

1393 Robson St., Vancouver, BC V6E 1C6
604-683-4558
Inexpensive—$40-$50 (Canadian); $5 per extra person; children under 16
free
MC, V

Directions: I-5 to Canada. Proceed north to Vancouver on Hwy 99, crossing over the Granville Bridge. Turn left on Nelson, right on Burrard, left on Robson. Located ½ mile north of downtown, on the way to Stanley Park.

At A Glance: Cribs; Kitchens; TV

The Greenbriar Apts. are a good choice of lodging if you don't care about being fancy, want to have the option of cooking your own meals, and would like to be centrally located for both downtown Vancouver (a half-mile walk) and Stanley Park (five minutes by bus or car). Rooms are large, and in addition to a separate bedroom, there is a living room with a hide-a-bed and a kitchenette. Underground free parking is available for patrons.

There are many grocery stores, fast food restaurants, ice cream places, ethnic restaurants and bakeries within easy walking distance of the motel.

Comments
"This is a good value, but it's just accommodations—comfortable and clean, but slightly tacky."

Whistler

Two hours driving time north of Vancouver on Highway 99 is the mountain resort community of Whistler. The British Columbia Railway makes daily runs from North Vancouver. In just 17 years Whistler has grown from a day-ski area to an international resort with hotels, lodges, condominiums, restaurants, shops, an 18-hole golf course, tennis courts, horseback riding, five lovely little lakes for swimming and boating, walking trails, hiking tours and more. It is a four-season resort best known for its winter sports, but like Sun Valley it is increasingly popular in summer.

Whistler Village Inn

P.O. Box 190, Whistler, BC V0N 1B0
604-932-4004
Moderate to Expensive—$55-$136 (Canadian); children under 12 free; ski package plans
AE, MC, V

Directions: I-5 north to Vancouver, then Hwy 99 to Whistler Village.

At A Glance: Kitchens; TV; Restaurant; Outdoor pool; Sauna; Hot tubs; Tennis courts; Hiking trails; Skiing; Organized activities for kids (skiing)

One of several places to stay in Whistler Village, the Whistler Village Inn offers more reasonable rates than places like Tantalus and The Delta Mountain Inn. The units are studios or have an extra sleeping loft in addition to the living room with hide-a-bed and kitchen. Quarters are a little crowded but efficient and very conveniently located. It's only a one- or two-block walk to the lift lines.

Skiing is great at Whistler from Thanksgiving to May, and in addition to cross-country areas, there's an immense area of runs for all levels of downhill skiers. In fact, the longest vertical drop in North America can be found at Whistler. Special programs with ski lessons for children are available if parents want to go off and ski by themselves. The heated pool and hot tub are a treat after skiing.

A great restaurant for kids in the Village is Peter's Underground. It's cafeteria style and inexpensive, with the kind of food that appeals to children. Send the kids there while you go to Umberto's, the best restaurant in the Village. Be sure to call and get reservations.

Comments

"We contended with MTV all weekend."

"If you're a skiing family, Whistler is wonderful because it's so accessible. And Canadians are extremely friendly and fun. *And* your dollar really buys a lot. One of the biggest advantages is that children under 12 pay only $7 ($5 U.S.) for a lift ticket. We have three kids and saved a lot of money."

Victoria

Victoria, population 64,000, is the capital of British Columbia on Vancouver Island. It is said to be more British than Great Britain. This far-off part of England has a gentle, sunny environment that breeds an easy lifestyle associated with flowers, gardens, double-decker London buses, cricket in the park, afternoon tea, antique shops and stately government buildings. Flower baskets hang from five-bubble lamp standards on city streets. The waterfront is always just a short walk away.

If you arrive on the Princess Marguerite steamer from Seattle, or the "Spirit of Friendship" jetfoil that runs between Seattle, Vancouver and Victoria, or the Black Ball ferry from Port Angeles, you will dock in the Inner Harbor just a short walk from the ivy-covered Empress Hotel where high tea has been served for seven decades to notables and commoners alike. Victoria is very walkable. The must-see world-famous Butchart Gardens are out of town but only a short drive by car or bus.

There are guided walking tours, guided tours on double-decker buses from London and rides in horse-drawn Tallyho carriages. The visitors' bureau at 812 Wharf Street has maps.

Favorite tourist attractions include Anne Hathaway's Cottage, the Classic Car Museum, Craigdarroch Castle, Crystal Garden, Fable Cottage Estate, Royal London Wax Museum, Sealand, Miniature World, the Provincial Museum and the All Fun Recreation Park. Victoria is at the southern tip of Vancouver Island. "Up Island" is worth visiting. If you are driving you can visit a number of interesting towns to the north and take a ferry across to the mainland from one of several points, Sidney, Nanaimo, Comox or Campbell River.

HOW TO GET THERE

To Victoria by car you may take the Black Ball ferry departing from Port Angeles (see Olympic Peninsula section) or drive to just south of Vancouver and follow Route 17 to Tsawwassen where the ferry departs for Sidney, 30 miles north of Victoria.

The steamer Princess Marguerite sails daily between Seattle and Victoria during summer months and the jetfoil Spirit of Friendship also has a schedule between Seattle, Victoria and Vancouver.

WHAT TO SEE ON THE WAY

If you are taking the ferry from Port Angeles to Victoria please refer to the Olympic Peninsula section. If you are taking the ferry from Anacortes to Sidney, B.C., please refer to the San Juan Islands section.

Oak Bay Beach Hotel

1175 Beach Drive, Victoria, BC V8S 2N2
604-598-4556
Moderate to Expensive—$49-$130 (Canadian); $12 per extra person
AE, MC, V

Directions: From the ferry terminal at Sidney, follow Rt. 17 south 32 miles to Victoria. Turn left on Fort, take a right on Oak Bay Ave. and follow it to Newport. Turn left on Windsor, right on Beach Dr. and follow to the hotel.

At A Glance: TV; Restaurant; Fishing rentals; Babysitting (by pre-arrangement)

The Oak Bay Beach Hotel bills itself as "Victoria's only seaside hotel." Located in the suburb of Oak Bay, the hotel has spacious, landscaped grounds that overlook the Strait of Georgia. The Tudor architecture is charming and the staff is friendly, but the place is a bit formal and probably better for families with older kids. If you don't mind having to drive the ten minutes into Victoria, this is a nice place to stay away from the hubbub of the city. There's a beautiful public beach less than a mile away, and if you bring your bikes you can explore the neighborhood with its mansions and lovely gardens.

The dining room is formal and expensive, and not a good idea for young children. High tea is served daily, and in warm weather it's on the veranda overlooking the water and grounds. Half a mile from the hotel is the Oak Bay Marina Restaurant, with moderate prices and excellent food. Children can go outside and look at the boats when they get restless. In addition, there are innumerable restaurants in Victoria proper.

Comments
"We heard the Provincial Museum in downtown Victoria was great, but our kids only wanted to hang out at the beach. They were dying to go on a charter fishing excursion ($59 family rate for 3½ hours)."

Oak Bay Beach Hotel

Royal Scot Motor Inn

425 Quebec St., Victoria, BC V8V 1W7
604-388-5463
Moderate—Summer: $52-$84 (Canadian); $10 per extra person;
Winter: $40-$57; $8 per extra person
AE, MC, V

Directions: In Victoria, the motel is located adjacent to Parliament Buildings and harbor.

At A Glance: Cribs; Kitchens; TV; Restaurant; Indoor pool; Sauna; Hot tub; Babysitting (by pre-arrangement)

To get you in the right mood for a stay in Victoria, all of the employees at The Royal Scot wear beautiful kilts. The Inn itself is comfortable and new, and the landscaped grounds are quiet. Most of the 150 units include kitchens and living rooms. The indoor pool, shower area and hot tub are clean and nice, and there are coin operated washers and dryers for wet suits and other laundry. Older kids will like the game room.

In addition to the good value, The Royal Scot offers a great location for a stay in Victoria. Its situation right at the hub of the city makes everything that this wonderful city has to offer within easy walking distance.

For tea and crumpets, try the James Bay Teahouse, located a couple of blocks from the Royal Scot.

Comments

"The service was wonderful, right down to our beds being turned down while we were at dinner with mints on our pillows and our daughter's stuffed animals all tucked in."

"We found it to be an excellent value."

Salt Spring Island

Salt Spring Island is the largest of the Gulf Island group lying between Vancouver Island and Vancouver on the mainland. The island has a relaxed, rural atmosphere which makes it popular with families for poking around the quaint villages, hiking, swimming in a freshwater lake, golfing and boating.

HOW TO GET THERE

Ferries operate daily from Swartz Bay on Vancouver Island to Fulford Harbor on Salt Spring; from Crofton on Vancouver Island to Vesuvius Bay on Salt Spring; and from Tsawwassen on the mainland to Long Harbor on Salt Spring.

Green Acres

RR 1, Lang Rd., Ganges, BC V0N 1E0
604-537-2585
Moderate—$45 (Canadian) for a 1-bedroom cabin for 2, $270 a week;
$60 for a 2-bedroom cabin for up to 4, $360 a week; off-season rates
available
MC, V

Directions: There are several routes to Salt Spring Island. For this resort take the Tsawwassen ferry. At Salt Spring Island, take Long Harbor Rd. until it ends. Turn right at the stop sign, then left at sign "To Vesuvius." Go to the next stop sign and turn right at the Community Hall. Go north about 2 miles and there will be a sign for Green Acres. Turn left onto Lang Rd. and follow a ½ mile to the resort.

At A Glance: Cribs and high chairs; Kitchens; TV; Outdoor pool; Boats; Play yard; Babysitting (by pre-arrangement)

Though it takes a while to get to the Gulf Islands, the advantages are that the scenery is lovely and you can make reservations on the ferry, assuring your departure and return. Salt Spring Island, with its green hills and meadows, inland lakes and rocky coast, is definitely worth a visit. So too is Green Acres, a family oriented resort located on a lake. A two-bedroom cabin nicely suits a family, with its equipped kitchen, living room and porch. The furnishings aren't fancy, so you can relax with your kids there.

In the summer, the lake is warm enough for swimming, and there's a nice safe beach. The resort has boats available for the use of their guests for no charge. On the grounds are a picnic area and swings. If you're looking for more diverse activities, riding, tennis, golf and charter fishing are all available on Salt Spring Island.

Comments
"Kids are well tolerated and prevalent."

"The mood of Salt Spring Island is relaxed and rural. The Canadians are very hospitable at the motel and in the shops. Despite some rain, the weekends we have spent there have been very enjoyable and memorable."

Harrison Hot Springs

This well-known health and recreation resort is located at the foot of Harrison Lake, due east of Vancouver. There are hot mineral springs that offer a contrast to lake swimming. The beach is sandy. All kinds of boats are available for rent. There is a public golf course nearby. Hiking trails lead into the Sasquatch Mountains where the big gorilla-man creature has been reportedly sighted many times. This is also known as rock hound country for agates, jades, garnets and fossils.

HOW TO GET THERE

To Harrison Hot Springs, about 155 miles and 3½ hours from Seattle, take I-5 north. Just beyond Bellingham take Highway 539 to the Lynden cutoff to Highway 9 to Sumas. The border station is always open.

WHAT TO SEE ON THE WAY

Please refer to the Birch Bay section.

The Harrison Hotel

Harrison Hot Springs, BC V0M 1K0
1-800-421-0000; in Seattle: 682-1981
Moderate to Expensive—$70-$90 (Canadian); various mid-week specials
AE, DC, MC, V

Directions: I-5 north to Bellingham. Just past Bellingham, take Hwy 539 and follow it to the Lynden cut-off, Hwy 546. Turn left and take this road to Sumas, then follow it until it runs into Trans-Canada 1. Take the Rosedale Exit east, pick up BC 9 and go north through Agassiz to Harrison Hot Springs.

At A Glance: Cribs; Restaurant; Indoor pool; Outdoor pool; Hot tub; Tennis courts; Bicycle rentals; Golf; Hiking trails; Ski trails; Boat rentals; Playground; Pets OK (bungalows only); Babysitting (by pre-arrangement); Organized activities for kids

The Harrison is located on the south shore of Harrison Lake, and most of the 285 units have views. Accommodations vary, but the best bets for families with children are rooms in the main building or the addition known as the Tower or West Wing so that it isn't necessary to leave the building before and after indoor swims. The bungalows are a good choice in summer and if you want to bring a pet. Rooms are comfortable and pleasant.

In addition to the numerous water sports, golf and tennis, the hotel offers indoor entertainment too: hot mineral pools and a recreation room with a pool table and video games. A short hike of about two miles on the grounds is suitable for families with small children. In the summer and during holidays there are all-day organized activities for children 12 and under.

The hotel's Terrace Room and Copper Room welcome children, but the food is expensive and not of exceptional quality. Within the town of Harrison Hot Springs, there are a number of coffee shops, schnitzel and steak type restaurants. Breakfasts and lunches are more reasonable in town than in the hotel.

Comments

"The Harrison presents an ambience of formality—a pleasant change for many contemporary families."

"Kids 8-12 will enjoy the independence of walking through the small town with its one main street, watching the curling next door to the hotel, visiting the gift shop, recreation room, and participating in high tea."

Osoyoos-Penticton

This area on the Canada-U.S. border is called British Columbia's desert. Lying between the rugged Coast Mountains to the west and the Rockies to the east, there are sand and sagebrush but also warm, shallow lakes and bountiful orchards as you start at Osoyoos and go north in the Okanagan Valley. Osoyoos is a pleasant village on Lake Osoyoos. A noted landmark is the Touch of Holland Windmill on Highway 3, a replica of an 1816 Dutch windmill of which fewer than 100 are still operating in the Netherlands. There are living quarters on the ground floor, and upstairs stones grind grain into flour. There is also a water slide park in the area.

To the north, Highway 97 links the lakes of Osoyoos, Vaseux, Skaha, Okanagan, Wood and Kalamalka. Along the highway is a profusion of fruit stands selling local produce in season, cherries, peaches, plums, apples and pears. There are a number of wineries. The beach towns of Penticton, Summerland, Kelowna and Vernon all are pleasant places with great beaches, swimming, boating and fishing. The lake water is ideally warm in summer. The sunny climate also promotes water slide parks. There are seven of them. A nice easy float trip is the five miles down the river channel from Okanagan Lake to Skaha Lake. Old MacDonald's Farm at Kelowna is rural fun for city kids.

Canadians love a party. It seems there is a festival, carnival, jamboree or regatta every month beginning with Kelowna's Snofest in January, featuring ice racing, polar bear dip, snowmobiling and a snowy bathing suit contest. Penticton has its Mid-Winter Breakout in February. The week-long Cherry Fiesta in Osoyoos is in late June. Penticton's Peach Festival in late July features the second largest annual parade in British Columbia. The Square Dance Jamboree at Penticton in early August is the largest outdoor dance in North America. The same area has a grape harvest fiesta in September, and all the wine-making communities stage Grape Olympics featuring barrel rolling, barehanded grape crushing and wine tasting.

Although this area is 400 miles from Vancouver, it attracts hundreds of coast Canadians in summer months. It is easily accessible on Highway 97 from Wenatchee through Omak, Okanagan and Oroville in Washington's Okanagan Valley, but it is not crowded with Americans. It remains a choice area to be discovered by many.

HOW TO GET THERE
   To Osoyoos and the Okanagan Valley, take I-90 or U.S. 2 from the Seattle area to Wenatchee. Near Wenatchee take U.S. 97 north to the border station at Oroville. It is always open.

WHAT TO SEE ON THE WAY
   Please refer to the Lake Chelan and Methow Valley sections.

Desert Motor Inn

7702 62nd Ave. (Box 458), Osoyoos, BC V0H 1V0
604-495-6525
Moderate—$38-$74 (Canadian); $4 per extra person
MC, V

Directions: From Wenatchee pick up Hwy 97 and follow it north into Canada. Osoyoos is located 2 miles over the border, the motel is located on Hwy 3, on the lakeshore.

At A Glance: Cribs; Kitchens; TV; Restaurant; Outdoor pool; Boat rentals; Playground

This motel gets its name from a large stretch of desert sand on the east side of Osoyoos Lake that extends north to Skaha Lake and west along the Similkameen River. Osoyoos is often called "Canada's best kept secret"—it's a large Canadian resort area that is little known by vacationers from the U.S.

The motel itself has two levels and 48 units. It's centrally located, on the water, and service and comfort are adequate. Like most motels in the area, it's located on the roadway. July and August are the best months to visit Osoyoos, so that you can take advantage of all the water sports. Boat rentals include rowboats, canoes, paddle boats, ski boats and ski jets. If you don't like swimming in the lake, the motel has an outdoor pool.

The dining room at the motel overlooks the pool and serves an excellent buffet. Go when you're hungry. They do have high chairs and a children's menu.

Comments

"Canadian motels in this area are clean and adequate, but don't expect the comfort you get in U.S. units."

"The Desert Motor Inn was a good value for a large family."

WESTERN WASHINGTON

Birch Bay

This saltwater beach resort community, ten miles south of the Canadian border, is just two hours from Seattle. The shallow sandy tidal beach is ideal in summer months for children to swim or just frolic in the water. The Semiahmoo Sandspit County Park on the coastal site of a trading post of the last century contains restored buildings and a visitor center. Birch Bay State Park has some easy hiking trails. Nearby is an amusement park that features warm-water slides that loop into swimming pools. There are other play and game areas.

HOW TO GET THERE
Take I-5 north from Seattle. Turn west at Exit 270 beyond Ferndale.

WHAT TO SEE ON THE WAY
Mount Vernon is the largest city in the rich Skagit Valley. Dairying, vegetable farming, and bulb growing are major industries. Daffodil fields blooming in late March and early April, tulips the last half of April and iris in early May provide spectacular masses of color. The Washington Cheese company has an observation room to watch cheese being made. Samples. Phone (206)757-4514 for the schedule every day except Sunday.

Bellingham is a beautiful old city on Bellingham Bay discovered by the English explorer Captain George Vancouver in 1792. The city has many Victorian homes built by lumber and fishing barons early this century. The Georgia-Pacific Corporation offers tours illustrating paper making. Children under ten not allowed. Phone (206)733-4410. The forested campus of Western Washington University on a hill overlooking the city is worth seeing for a variety of contemporary sculptures.

Jacob's Landing

7824 Birch Bay Dr., Blaine, WA 98230
206-371-7633
Moderate—$55-$65 per night (accommodates 4-6); $300-$500 per week
MC, V

Directions: I-5 to Birch Bay, Exit 270. Go west 4 miles, left at third
stop sign, left on Birch Bay Dr. Located 2 miles north of state park.

At A Glance: Cribs; Kitchens; TV; Indoor pool; Hot tub; Tennis
courts; Racquetball courts; Babysitting (by pre-arrangement)

This is a beachfront condominium development with a pleasant ar-
chitectural style. Not all units have views, but all have decks, living
room, dining area, fireplace (but no wood), fully equipped kitchen and
bath. One- and two-bedroom units are available; two-bedroom units
have a queen bed in one room, twins in the other, plus a fold-out
couch in the living room. Sound insulation between the units is good.

The main thing that Jacob's Landing has to recommend it is its
location—a quick two hours from Seattle, and only 40 miles south of
Vancouver, B.C. The beach is located across the road and is rocky
and not particularly inviting, though the water is warm enough for
swimming in the summer. The indoor pool is a good option when the
weather is bad. There are lots of things to do nearby—golf, water-
slides, a roller skating rink, bike and moped rentals—so there is
plenty of activity if you leave the condominium complex itself. Jacob's
Landing is probably a good place to go if you need a change of scene
for the weekend or want to break up a longer trip, but you probably
wouldn't want to spend your entire summer vacation there.

San Juan Islands

This magnificent archipelago is close enough for brief holidays as well as protracted vacations. There are 172 islands in the San Juans. Two-thirds of the islands' 8900 residents live on San Juan, Orcas, Lopez and Shaw Islands, the only ones served by state ferries. On these islands you will find everything for a well-rounded vacation of outdoor activities and the comforts of good food and lodging.

Our recommended places are on Orcas and Lopez Islands. Although Orcas is larger, both islands have the same characteristics of quiet roads through rolling countryside dotted with old orchards and small farms. Nature is seen at close range. Deer are numerous and tame. The beaches are accessible. There is no difficulty in picking your own quiet lagoon on a sandy beach with lots of driftwood. Orcas, with its large Moran State Park topped by 2400-foot Mount Constitution, has two freshwater lakes for swimming, boating and fishing. Both islands are so ideal for bicycle touring there seem to be more bikes than automobiles once you leave the ferry landing areas. The towns are not large but are well-supplied to serve year-round residents.

HOW TO GET THERE

Unless you travel by private boat or plane you must ride a Washington State ferry to reach these islands. The ferry route is from Anacortes to Sidney, British Columbia. In Washington the ferry leaves from Anacortes, about 90 minutes north of Seattle. Take I-5 north about 60 miles to connect with Highway 20 west to the Anacortes-Sidney ferry terminal. To Lopez the ferry ride is about 60 minutes, to Orcas about 75 minutes.

The ferries are large and comfortable and offer food service. They are prepared to take all sorts of conveyances including canoes, bicycles, vans and trailers. The trip is a scenic feast as the ferry traverses narrow passages between islands, moves among a variety of smaller boats and ties up at picturesque landings.

Special note: If you are taking a car you must plan to be in line at

the boarding area in Anacortes considerably before sailing time if you
are traveling on a weekend in summer months. Check with the
Washington State Ferry System, (206)464-6400, or out-of-Seattle toll
free 1-800-542-0810, for current information.

In British Columbia, the ferry terminal is at Sidney, about 30 miles
north of Victoria on Vancouver Island.

WHAT TO SEE ON THE WAY

Wenberg State Park is an easy rest stop just off I-5 north of
Everett. An alternate route to Anacortes (turn off I-5 to Highway 534
south of Mount Vernon) through Conway and La Conner, a picturesque waterfront village near the Swinomish Indian Reservation,
provides a close look at a scenic dairy and farming area, part of the
Skagit Flats.

Beach Haven Resort

Rt. 1, Box 12, Eastsound, WA 98245
206-376-2288
Moderate—$29-$119
No credit cards

Directions: Take the ferry to Orcas Island, then drive to the north tip of the island and follow the signs.

At A Glance: Kitchens; Boat rentals

Beach Haven is located on the water, and the cabins are nestled in the woods. They're quite rustic but clean and comfortable with fireplaces and kitchens. Two of the cabins are large enough to accommodate two families or one large family. These have lots of rooms to get lost in and a wonderful view of the water.

Beach Haven is the kind of place where a family vacations *together*. There are no phones, TV, tennis courts, pool or other distractions. Bring your suits to swim in the sound, your cards, books and games to pass the evenings, and lots of popcorn! You can rent a rowboat or hike in the forest behind the resort.

You must travel some distance to shop or find a restaurant, but if you are out exploring the island and want some good suggestions for eating on Orcas, look under the Rosario listing below.

Comments
"This is a place for parents to relax and for kids to run free."

North Beach Inn

P.O. Box 80, Eastsound, WA 98245
206-376-2660
Moderate—$34-$75; $7 per extra person; weekly rates available; 15%
rate reduction off season
No credit cards

Directions: Take the ferry to Orcas Island. Head north as you exit
the ferry and follow the signs.

At A Glance: Cribs; Kitchens; Restaurant (summer only); Boat rentals; Pets OK

The eleven cottages of this resort are in a wooded setting bordering ⅓ mile of pebble beach. There are, in addition, 90 acres of woods and fields, and the view is towards the Canadian San Juans and sunsets. Cottages are simple but clean, and each has a fireplace. Bring your entertainment with you. This is a no-frills vacation spot designed to get the family together for some good beach scavenging or bird watching.

There is a dining room at the Inn. It is open only during the summer and serves breakfast and dinner with advance reservations. Meals

North Beach Inn

are simple and nourishing and the setting is well suited to families with children. For suggestions on restaurants on Orcas, see the Rosario listing below.

Comments

"The real fun is in building a fire on the beach at night. But beware—with all the fires over the years, playing in the sand can result in some pretty dirty legs and knees."

Rosario Resort

Eastsound, WA 98245
1-800-562-8820
Expensive—$75-$99; $7 per extra person; $10 per roll-away; children under 12 free
AE, MC, V

Directions: Take the ferry to Orcas Island. Follow signs to Eastsound, and from there to the resort.

At A Glance: Cribs ($4); Kitchens; TV; Indoor pool; Outdoor pools (2); Hot tub; Sauna; Lawn games; Tennis courts; Boat rentals; Playground; Babysitting (management will provide a list); Car rentals

Rosario is a large place—190 units, built on an old estate overlooking Cascade Bay. Units vary in their appointments—some have kitchens, some fireplaces, some are in the main lodge—and all are uniformly well-maintained. Built by a shipping magnate at the turn of the century, the huge old lodge, Moran Mansion, has lovely mahogany woodwork. The grounds are spread out and provide lots of lawn space for horsing around. There are two outdoor swimming pools. One of these pools is for adults only and is more for dipping than swimming. The larger pool is for families but there is no lifeguard. There is an indoor pool that's fun for older kids but uniformly deep, and thus probably not good for smaller children.

The dining room at Rosario's is not truly formal, but it's not casual either. A better choice for kids is the Surfsider Snack and Deli, which is right next to the marina. The price is right and the atmosphere is relaxed. If you leave the resort, you'll find several decent restaurants in Eastsound. La Famiglia Ristorante on A Street serves excellent Italian food and has children's portions and high chairs. There's a large deck for eating outside, too. Reservations are needed. Bilbo's, also on A Street, serves Mexican food and has a menu "por los niños." In the Sears Building you'll find The Villager, a casual family spot with good burgers. There's an outside deck and a swing set next to it. On the night you get a sitter, try Christina, a small, lovely, romantic restaurant overlooking the water. And finally, when you're ready to go home and you've parked your car in the line for the ferry at Orcas Landing, go to The Old Orcas Hotel. They serve gourmet burgers and a country-style breakfast and provide high chairs.

Comments

"The tap water was too hot."

"You really need a car. The resort is on the water at the bottom of a long and steep hill, so it's not easy to hike out. There are so many things to do away from the resort that unless you are hearty walkers or bicyclists you'll want a car."

"We saw many deer."

The Islander Lopez

P.O. Box 197, Lopez, WA 98261
206-468-2233
Moderate—$40-$70; $10 per extra person 13 and over; reduced rates
off-season
AE, MC, V

Directions: Take the ferry to Lopez Island. From the ferry terminal, drive 5 miles to the motel, located on Fisherman's Bay.

At A Glance: Cribs; Kitchens; TV; Restaurant; Outdoor pool (summer only); Hot tub; Bicycle rentals; Fishing rentals; Boat rentals; Playground; Babysitting (by pre-arrangement)

The Islander Lopez offers 32 rooms and four cabins. Some are equipped with kitchens, almost all have an unobstructed sunset view. The motel is located on Fisherman's Bay, so if you arrive by boat you can moor right at one of the Islander's slips. If you've come, like so many people do, to ride bikes along the quiet country roads of this island, the Islander is a good place to rest overnight and put your feet up.

The Islander Lopez restaurant, located across the street from the motel, serves a continental breakfast and typical American fare. Seafood is fresh and the view is good, but sometimes there's a long wait for dinner. Another choice, about a mile down the road in Lopez, is the New Bay Cafe. Kids are well tolerated and high chairs are available at this simple, pleasant restaurant.

Comments

"The Islander is a very comfortable, pleasant motel. The people were very friendly and helpful. The style is late quasi-Polynesian: bamboo and fishing nets abound in the restaurant. Rooms are simply furnished and clean."

"The beach access and the restaurant are across a road from some of the units, so children need supervision."

Whidbey Island

This second largest of all islands in the continental United States offers one of the easiest getaways. While not far from the Seattle metropolitan area it has a distinctive island flavor disconnected from mainland existence. The southern half of the island, below Coupeville, is different from the more populated Oak Harbor area at the north end. Because the island is connected to the mainland by a spectacular bridge across Deception Pass north of Oak Harbor, a visit to Whidbey Island can be a circle tour.

Exploring Whidbey Island is a varied experience. It is a long, narrow island with miles and miles of beaches to choose from. Six state parks offer a range of trees, beach, history and wildlife. The two standouts are Fort Casey on the west side opposite Coupeville and Deception Pass State Park at the north end. Fort Casey was once an army installation with big guns guarding Puget Sound. The open parade grounds and the concrete bunkers, some with immobilized guns, give youngsters a great chance to run and climb free of "don'ts." It has great beaches, picnic areas and trails.

Deception Pass State Park has freshwater Cranberry Lake right next to a salt water beach. There are easy mountain trails to hike, beautiful mountain and sea vistas, and good camping facilities.

Most of the towns of Whidbey Island have maintained their characteristics which have attracted writers and artists and individuals with open life styles. Langley has the largest and most varied art colony. The Clyde Theater in Langley shows a good selection of new movies and occasionally offers stage shows performed by talented locals. Art and craft fairs abound in summer months. The Island County Fair at Langley in August is an old-fashioned grass-roots affair—great fun.

Coupeville is more touristy. The harbor buildings have been restored. Good antique shopping.

HOW TO GET THERE
Take I-5 north to Exit 189 to Highway 525 turnoff, marked

Mukilteo-Whidbey Island ferry. From Seattle to the ferry terminal is 28 miles. Ferries run on the hour and half-hour. The crossing to Clinton takes 20 minutes. Follow Highway 525 which runs the length of the island.

A second ferry route runs from Keystone on Whidbey Island to Port Townsend on the Olympic Peninsula. To reach Keystone turn off Highway 525 near Coupeville.

WHAT TO SEE ON THE WAY

Highway 525 passes the Boeing Everett plant where the famous 747 jumbo jet and the 767 are assembled in the largest building in the world. It's a fascinating 90-minute tour, weekdays only. Children 11 and under cannot tour the plant but can watch the 45-minute program at the Tour Center which begins with an eight-minute film that shows how 3 million separate pieces are put together in two months to make a jet airliner. To reach the Tour Center drive past the main assembly building and watch for the Tour Center sign on the right. Tour times are available by calling Everett Public Tours (206)342-4801.

Mutiny Bay Resort Motel

P.O. Box 249, Freeland, WA 98249
206-321-4500
Inexpensive to Moderate—$30-$60; $5 per extra person; weekly rates
available
MC, V

Directions: From Clinton, drive 10 miles on Hwy 525 to Freeland.
Turn left on Fish Rd and proceed 1 mile to end of road; resort drive-
way is to your right.

At A Glance: Kitchens; TV; Sport court; Pets OK off season

Mutiny Bay Resort offers both chalets and cabins. The four chalets
($60) are situated right on the beach. Each has three bedrooms, a
fireplace in the living room, a complete kitchen with dining area and a
lanai. They are carpeted and have sliding glass doors that give direct
access to the beach. Cabins ($30), simply decorated and furnished,
are set back in the trees and have two bedrooms, a small living room
with a hide-a-bed and a kitchenette. There are no showers or tubs in
the cabins, but during the summer guests can use the showers
provided in the camping area. (RV hook-ups are available.)

The beach in front of the resort is small but good for clamming and
shell collecting, and there's a long fishing dock. In the summer you
can swim in the bay. There is a small yard for ball games, as well as
a sport court, and the owner has a box of pails and toys that are
available on loan.

Comments

"We were pleased with the resort as a close, simple weekend
'getaway.' The owners are cordial and helpful."

"We liked being there in the fall when there weren't any campers
around. It was fairly quiet and peaceful, and a real bargain."

The Orchard Bed & Breakfast

619 Third St., Langley, WA 98260
206-221-7880
Moderate—$40-$70 nightly; $210-$350 weekly
No credit cards

Directions: From Clinton follow Highway 525 to the Langley turnoff on the right.

At A Glance: Cradle; TV; Breakfast; Bicycles; Play yard; Babysitting (by pre-arrangement)

The Orchard Bed and Breakfast

The Orchard is that rare thing—a charming bed and breakfast that welcomes children. The $70 rate is for two bedrooms and a renovated bath for a family of four. The old, remodeled farmhouse is open seven days a week in the summer from mid-June to Labor Day, weekends only the rest of the year. Parents can sit on the porch swing while children play in the large yard, an old orchard with good trees for climbing equipped with swings and ropes. Tunnels through the bramble bushes make great hideouts. Guests can pick berries and help themselves to fruits and nuts off the trees. The Orchard is close to the beach and to a school playground. For rainy days the owner has lots of children's books and games. She can also recommend good babysitters for kids of any age.

Breakfast at The Orchard is a big continental: juice, coffee, tea or milk, pastries, whole-grain breads, fresh fruits, and homemade jams and preserves. A good restaurant for kids, within walking distance of The Orchard, is Al's Place, on the main street in Langley. Al's has good service, a relaxed atmosphere, high chairs and good food— burgers, sandwiches, a salad bar, beer and wine. If you want to get a babysitter or if your children are older and/or civilized, try Michael's Your Place, 30 miles away in Coupeville, which offers a combination of funky island hospitality, big-city prices and delicious food.

Comments

"This is a different but enriching experience for families: not as anonymous as a hotel nor as private as a cabin or motel, but interesting. Martha Murphy goes out of her way to make families comfortable and is a great resource for things to do in the area. She has two children and so is quite realistic about a family's needs."

Kitsap Peninsula

This is a crooked finger of the mainland that rests in the middle of Puget Sound between the Tacoma-Seattle-Everett area to the east and Hood Canal to the west. The two recommended places, The Last Resort on Puget Sound near Hansville and Alderbrook Inn on Hood Canal near Union, are at the north and south extremes of the peninsula.

The north end of the peninsula holds many charming reminders of days past. There is a fine new museum on the Suquamish Indian Reservation on Agate Pass, "The Eyes of Chief Seattle," full of "hands-on" artifacts. This is where Chief Seattle resided and where he is buried. In the same area is the Little Boston Indian Reservation of the Klallam Indians, a small, self-contained community with some exceptional totem poles. The Foulweather Bluff lighthouse is picturesque. At Point No Point in 1855, Isaac Stevens, later governor of the state, signed an important treaty with ten Indian tribes. Only 30 minutes away is Poulsbo, a "little Norway" community of fishermen. It is sparkling clean and old country. Port Gamble near the Hood Canal Floating Bridge offers a stroll in the last century. Two Maine lumbermen, Pope and Talbot, founded the town in 1853 and it has been preserved as a 19th century community ever since. Many Victorian-style homes, churches and buildings have been restored. The tree-lined streets are lighted by gas lamps. The sawmill is one of the oldest operating in the country.

At the south end of the peninsula the environment is dominated by Hood Canal, a long stretch of quiet seawater that deadends near Union. The canal is rich in shrimp, oysters and fish. The winding road along the canal is dotted with shops and stores featuring home crafts, good food and idyllic scenery. Summer is a special time for swimming when the salt water of the canal warms up.

HOW TO GET THERE

From Seattle the north Kitsap area can be reached by either of two routes taking about 90 minutes, including a ferry crossing. Usually the quickest way is north about seven miles on I-5 to Exit 177 to the Edmonds-Kingston Ferry. At Kingston, stay on Highway 104 for two miles and then turn north eight miles to Hansville. An alternate route is the Seattle-Winslow ferry from downtown Seattle to Bainbridge Island. Stay on Highway 305 across the Agate Pass Bridge, then turn north through Suquamish and follow the signs to Hansville.

The south Hood Canal area is most easily reached by taking the Seattle-Bremerton ferry from downtown Seattle. The travel time is 55 minutes on the ferry and 50 minutes driving. At Bremerton follow Highway 3 to Belfair. Beyond Belfair turn right on Highway 106 toward Union, approximately 13 miles to Alderbrook Inn.

WHAT TO SEE ON THE WAY

Some area attractions in north Kitsap are described above.

On the way to the south end of Hood Canal the biggest attraction is the Puget Sound Naval Base at Bremerton, including the Puget Sound Naval Shipyard. The star of the mothballed fleet, the U.S.S. Missouri, has been towed away to be reactivated, but there are others to see.

Alderbrook Inn Resort

E. 7101 Hwy 106, Union, WA 98592
206-622-2404 or 206-621-1119 (direct Seattle lines) or 206-898-2200
Moderate to Expensive—Rooms $58-$63; 2-bedroom cottages $80, or
$90 if waterfront ($5 per additional person over 4); children under 12
free
AE, MC, V

Directions: I-5 south to Olympia, then Hwy 101 north, bypassing
Shelton. Turn right on Hwy 106 just before Potlatch and follow it for
7 miles to the resort. Or, take Seattle-Bremerton ferry and follow
signs for 304 W.to Belfair and Shelton to get out of the city, then follow Hwy 3S to Belfair. Turn right on Hwy 106W and follow 13 miles
to the resort.

At A Glance: Cribs; Kitchens; TV; Game room; Restaurant; Indoor
pool; Sauna; Hot tub; Lawn games; Golf; Tennis courts; Boat rentals;
Playground; Babysitting (by pre-arrangement)

This is a resort that's a good choice for a getaway any time of the
year. In the summer, the water in Hood Canal is pleasantly warm for
swimming and there's a big dock at Alderbrook with a wonderful slide
into the canal. Colder seasons are also fine, as the large pool and hot
tubs are covered. If you want to sail or boat to Alderbrook, you can
moor your boat there. If your nautical aspirations are less, paddle-
boats can be rented and are easily maneuvered by young children.

Alderbrook, situated on 525 wooded acres on the shores of Hood
Canal, has views of the Olympic Mountains. There are 102 accommodations: 79 guest rooms with lanais; 21 two-bedroom cottages with
equipped kitchenettes and fireplaces; and two conference suites.

The resort's Beachside dining room has a good, inexpensive children's menu for kids under 12. Food and service are good and high
chairs are available. If you want to find food off the resort grounds,
try the Union Cafe, two miles away in—you guessed it—Union. It's a
smoky tavern atmosphere but there's local color, the food is fine and
kids love it. Dinner is less than $6 per meal.

Comments

"The short trip from Seattle to Alderbrook is easy for kids. The
ferry ride is like one giant stop for children—they can run, snack, look
for whales. The driving route up the canal is short and lovely."

The Last Resort

2546 N.E. Twin Spits Rd., Hansville, WA 98340
206-638-2358
*Inexpensive to Moderate—Cottages $43 a day, $260 a week, $180 for 5
nights (Sun-Thurs); main house $64 a day, $385 a week, $270 for 5
nights; $4 per extra person; winter rates approximately 20% less
No credit cards*

Directions: From Hansville go 3½ miles out Twin Spits Rd. One
hundred yards after Dead End sign, take sharp left into Last Resort.
Small sign is on mailbox on right side of road.

At A Glance: Kitchens; Outdoor pool (summer only); Pets considered

This is a funky, unpretentious resort that is clean and well maintained. Cottages have two very small bedrooms, each with a double
bed. The Main House has three bedrooms with a queen bed, a double, and a pair of twins as well as large living and dining rooms. Kitchens and bathrooms are well appointed and there are wood stoves.
The management supplies linens, towels, blankets and firewood.

The setting is beautiful and you're on your own for entertainment.
The huge saltwater beach is great for playing in the sand, throwing
rocks, identifying abundant sea life, walking barefoot on the tide flats
and building beach fires. There is a large grassy area for frisbees,
soccer, etc. The heated outdoor pool at the resort is open only in the
summer. If you like winter storms and have warm raingear, you might
enjoy The Last Resort in the winter.

There are no restaurants nearby. "It's best to bring your own
food," says the owner. "This place thinks it's an island and the
stores charge island prices."

Comments

"The only diversions are the beach and pool. Probably not good for
kids over ten. This is a place for parents who want to interact with
their children on vacation. Not recommended for parents who need a
break from their kids."

Olympic Peninsula

The Olympic Peninsula is a 7215-square-mile area between the Pacific Ocean and Hood Canal encompassing examples of about every kind of geography, wildlife and climate to be found in the entire state. Rainfall varies from 15 inches annually in the sunny banana belt at Sequim on the north side to a perpetually moist 200 inches in the rain forests of Olympic National Park. It is a richly endowed chunk of nature, too much to be digested at one time. Fortunately it is reasonably close to the Seattle metropolitan area. In two hours driving time you can be nibbling away at it.

The northeast side of the peninsula along Hood Canal and the Strait of Juan de Fuca is the most heavily populated. Port Townsend with a year-round population of about 6000 is called the Victorian seaport and is a national historic landmark. There are more than 70 Victorian residences, buildings, old forts, parks and monuments. Many commercial buildings have been restored and contain shops offering the work of local painters, sculptors, weavers, potters, poets and writers. Fort Worden State Park was the location for filming of "An Officer and a Gentleman."

While Port Townsend capitalizes on the past, Port Angeles, about 40 miles to the west, is a bustling city of 17,000 with a big timber industry, lumber and paper mills and fishing. ITT Rayonier offers pulp mill tours. Phone (206)457-3391 for information.

In between Port Townsend and Port Angeles is Sequim (pronounced Skwim), blessed with the driest coastal area north of Southern California. Many of the 3000 residents are retired. A special attraction is the Manis Mastodon Site where a team of archeologists from Washington State University is collecting evidence that early man hunted mastodons, a primitive form of elephant now extinct. The site is open from June through Labor Day, except Monday. Also nearby is the Olympic Game Farm, a 90-acre preserve for animals used in many wildlife films and television shows. The farm was formerly owned by Walt Disney Studios. Walking tours include movie sets, descriptions of

film-making, opportunities to pet some of the animals and sometimes
to see them perform. There are also self-guided driving tours. The
farm is open June 1-September 30.

On the waterfront is Dungeness Spit, six miles long, extending into
the Strait of Juan de Fuca. It is one of the longest natural sandspits in
the country and forms a part of a wildlife refuge to shelter more than
250 species of waterfowl and shorebirds.

One of the fringe benefits of traveling in this area is access to superb seafood. Salmon, crabs, oysters and clams are abundant. You
can get your own within state regulations, buy them in markets or eat
them in places that specialize in whatever is seasonally available.

As for the mountains, Port Angeles is a good entry point to Olympic National Park. An easy introduction to this vast area is a 20-mile
drive to Hurricane Ridge, a high country vantage point 5200 feet
above sea level. Naturalist programs with films and exhibits are held
daily from July 1 through Labor Day and again on weekends from mid-
December until mid-April, the skiing season. Majestic views of mountains, glaciers, forests, flowers and wildlife vary from plain grand in
any kind of weather to super-spectacular on clear days. There are 600
miles of trails, some easy and others safe only for experienced hikers.
Wildlife abounds. The elk population is estimated at 5000. Blacktail
deer and smaller mammals are common. The park is open all year,
but snow sometimes restricts access to the high country. Current information is available at the visitor center in Port Angeles.

U.S. 101 circles the park and the adjoining Olympic National Forest.
Just west of Port Angeles there is a side road up the Elwha River for
five miles. A two-hour raft trip between Lake Mills and Lake Aldwell
is an out-of-the-ordinary diversion.

Farther along on U.S. 101 is Lake Crescent, a ten-mile stretch of
water that may be the most beautiful forest-water setting you will
ever see.

Beyond the lake a paved road branches off to go 14 miles up the
Soleduck River through forest primeval. There are many trails and
picnic areas and at road's end is Sol Duc Hot Springs Resort offering
swimming and soaking in pools of naturally heated mineral water.

Back on U.S. 101 the road passes through several logging towns.
Timber is king in this region. The giant log-loaded trucks go whizzing
past as numerous as taxis in downtown Seattle.

There are ten Indian tribal nations on the peninsula. The Washington Coast section of this book covers several of them. At Sappho
there is a turnoff to a ten-mile road connecting with Highway 112 that
leads to Neah Bay on the coast, a fishing town of 1500 Makah Indians. There is a good museum and numerous places to buy carvings
and baskets from their makers.

A trip to this part of the Olympic Peninsula without seeing one of the rain forests would be unthinkable. Easiest to reach is the Hoh Rain Forest 18 miles up the Hoh River from Highway 101. There is a visitor center with complete information about the trail through the Hall of Mosses and other delightful sights. Walking among giant 250-year-old Sitka spruce trees is a date with Mother Nature not soon forgotten. There are also raft trips on the Hoh River and the Queets River. The Queets is farther south on Highway 101, after it hugs the coast line for 18 miles from Ruby Beach to south of Kalaloch. This area is described in the Washington Coast section of this book.

About 25 miles after the highway turns east is the other noted lake in the park, Lake Quinault, the jumping-off place for the Quinault Rain Forest. The rustic Lake Quinault Lodge appears much the same as it was in 1937 when President Franklin D. Roosevelt visited to see first-hand the proposed national park.

From Lake Quinault, Highway 101 turns south to Hoquiam, where it joins Highway 12 leading to Highway 8, Olympia, Tacoma and Seattle.

HOW TO GET THERE

The most direct routes from Seattle are the Seattle-Winslow ferry and the Edmonds-Kingston ferry (I-5 north to Exit 177). After the ferry crossing follow signs to the Hood Canal Floating Bridge which is on Highway 104. Follow this to U.S. 101. If Lake Quinault or Kalaloch is your destination, take I-5 south to Olympia, taking the U.S. 101 turnoff to connect with Highway 8 to Aberdeen. This becomes Highway 12.

From Portland take U.S. 30 north along the Columbia River to Astoria. Take the toll bridge across the Columbia from Astoria to Megler. Follow U.S. 101 to Aberdeen-Hoquiam. Continue north on U.S. 101 to circle the Olympic Pennisula.

WHAT TO SEE ON THE WAY

Please see the Kitsap Peninsula section of this book for suggestions of things to see on the way to the Olympic Peninsula.

The Ecologic Place

10 Beach Drive, Nordland, WA 98358
206-385-3077
Moderate—$30-$75 per cabin per night; weekly rates $180-$450
No credit cards

Directions: From Hood Canal Bridge take Hwy 104 to Chimacum. Follow signs to Hadlock, then to Indian Island/Nordland/Ft. Flagler. After crossing Indian Island, watch for the "Welcome to Marrowstone Island" sign. Turn right and The Ecologic Place is just ahead on the right.

At A Glance: Cribs; Kitchens; Canoe rentals

The eleven rustic cedar cabins, situated around a lodge in a meadow above the beach, vary in size and accommodate from two to six guests each. The cabins, which have relatively new bathrooms, kitchens and wood stoves, are equipped with linens, towels, dishes and basic utensils. You must bring extra blankets or sleeping bags for warmth at night in cool weather. Cabins have views of Oak Bay and the Olympic mountains to the west and Mt. Rainier to the southeast, and they are available by the week, weekend, or midweek special. During July and August, only children eight years and younger are accepted.

The Ecologic Place is a good place to relax—to ride bikes, walk or play on the three miles of driftwood-strewn beach, explore the salt marsh. To water-wise guests who sign a release, the management will rent a canoe. Indoors, the lodge has a supply of books, board games and a piano.

Comments

"The Ecologic Place is very quiet and designed to meld into the natural surroundings. The idea is to make your own fun. If you are looking for organized activities this is not the spot to go."

"The cabins were very clean and had attractive touches like interesting wall hangings and fresh-cut flowers."

Fort Worden State Park

Port Townsend, WA 98368
206-385-4730
Moderate—$45-$146 per house
No credit cards

Directions: Located 1 mile north of Port Townsend. Well marked.

At A Glance: Kitchens; Cafeteria; Tennis courts; Fishing rentals

Fort Worden State Park is a 330-acre park located on wooded hillsides overlooking the Strait of Juan de Fuca. Eighteen stately two-story houses, once officers' quarters at the turn of the century, house visitors. Most of the houses are completely refurbished, with carpeting and reproductions of Victorian furniture. Those that have not been refurbished are comfortable with good beds and fireplaces. Bed linens and towels are provided, and the houses are heated so are comfortable all year. All kitchens are large and fully equipped. Most of the houses are large enough for two families (or even three) to share, which brings the cost well into the "inexpensive" range.

Fort Worden is a fine place for a family to bring their bikes. The beach is good for romping, but the water is too cold for swimming. The highlight is the old fort itself, complete with gunmounts, bunkers and cliffs to explore. On a cultural note, the Celebration of American Arts, a ten-week series of workshops, symposia and festival performances with nationally acclaimed musicians, visual artists, dancers and literary figures, is held each summer at the park.

If you don't feel like cooking every meal, you can get one at the cafeteria with advance notice. Or, a short trip into Port Townsend to Lido By the Sea, 2500 Washington St., will give you a moderately priced meal. It's a fun and friendly place, and noisy enough that kids are not a problem.

Comments
"A great value."

"When our friends left, we were alone in the huge Ft. Worden house. It was stormy and quite spooky."

Lake Crescent Lodge

Star Rte. 1, Box 11, Port Angeles, WA 98362
206-928-3211
Moderate—$35-$55; $5 per extra person
MC, V

Directions: Located 25 miles west of Port Angeles on U.S. 101

At A Glance: Cribs; Restaurant; Boat rentals; Hiking trails; Pets OK

This national park concession is open only from Memorial Day to September 30. Lake Crescent is magnificent in the summer. The color of the water varies from turquoise to green. On very warm days, swimming in the cold water can be exhilarating and there's a nice beach at the lodge. For warmer swimming, it's not too far to drive to the hot springs at Sol Duc.

The lodge, motel units along the shore, and cabins are clean and nicely furnished. Many of the guests are older, but families are welcome. In addition to swimming, families can boat, fish from the dock, go on short hikes, or just use the facility as a base for excursions into the Olympic National Park.

The restaurant at the lodge has moderate prices and high chairs, but the food is mediocre. Try instead the Log Cabin Resort Restaurant on Eastbank Rd., eight miles from Lake Crescent Lodge. The food is moderately expensive, but it's good and the beautiful location and nice atmosphere make it worth the trip.

Comments

"After camping in the rain Lake Crescent Lodge looked very nice for a couple of nights."

Lake Quinault Lodge

South Shore Rd., P.O. Box 7, Quinault, WA 98575
1-800-562-6672 in Washington; 206-288-2571
Moderate—$39-$70 per night; $6 per extra person over 6 years old, $3
if under 6; lots of package "deals."
MC, V

Directions: Follow U.S. 101 40 miles north of Hoquiam. Take the
Lake Quinault South Shore Recreational Area Exit. Follow the South
Shore Rd. two miles to the lodge.

At A Glance: Cribs ($3); Restaurant; Indoor pool; Hot tub; Sauna;
Game room; Hiking trails; Nature programs (spring and summer);
Lawn games (spring and summer); Boat rentals (spring and summer);
Playground; Pets OK ($5 per night in Lakeside Inn only); Babysitting
(by pre-arrangement).

The setting of this lodge, on a beautiful lake in the middle of the
rain forest, is one of the best on the Olympic Peninsula. The lobby of
the main lodge, with its huge fireplace, is quaint—lots of old wood and
Indian art. The least expensive rooms, located in the main lodge,
either share a bathroom between two rooms or have no bath, with facilities down the hall. Some of these rooms have views of the parking
lot rather than the lake. Lakeside Inn rooms, built in 1923 and recently remodeled, have private baths. Newer yet are the "gas fireplace
units," which offer a queen size bed and a queen hide-a-bed. The
lodge offers lots of special deals—mid-week, off-season, etc., but
there is a two-night minimum on weekends and a three-night minimum
on holiday weekends and school vacations.

Lake Quinault Lodge is obviously geared to families. Adjacent to the
pool there is a game room with equipment for horseshoes, volleyball,
frisbee and badminton, as well as pinball, ping pong and video games,
pop and candy machines. Hiking trails through the rain forest of 0.5,
1.6 and 3.0 miles start at the lodge; maps are at the front desk. Also
at the front desk are lobby games, puzzles, arrangements for sitters,
and even rubber sheets for bed-wetters. Nature programs and canoe
and rowboat rentals ($2 an hour) are available in the summer. The
playground has swings, a slide, see-saw and rings.

The dining room, located in the main lodge, has good food, nice
personnel, and slow service. Window seats are the best because you
can watch the hummingbirds feed. A good alternative to using the
restaurant is the bar, which offers carry-out sandwiches and drinks.

Alternatives to eating at Quinault are extremely limited but there is
one spot: the Amanda Park Cafe, near the junction of the South Shore

Recreation Exit and Highway 101. The cafe, which is frequented by locals and loggers, has high chairs and reasonable prices. Best of all, service is friendly and they're nice to kids.

Comments

"The service in the restaurant was incredibly pleasant and incredibly slow. Waiters and waitresses are *very* nice to kids, but the setting is difficult. The gift shop is located right with the restaurant: millions of breakables are begging to be broken by curious little hands."

"A nice place for kids—you don't have to worry about them ruining beige carpets."

"Our kids really liked the antique cars parked out front."

Lake Quinault Lodge

The Resort at Port Ludlow

781 Walker Way, Port Ludlow, WA 98365
1-800-732-1239 or 206-437-2222
Expensive—$58-$95 for bedroom and bath; $115 and up for
1-4-bedroom apartments; winter rates slightly less; several package
"deals;" children under 12 free in parents' room.
AE, CB, DC, MC, V

Directions: From the Hood Canal Bridge: turn right on Paradise Bay Rd. and go to the stop sign (6 miles). Turn right on Oak Bay Rd. Resort is on the right in ½ mile.

At A Glance: Cribs (free); Kitchens; TV; Game room; Restaurant; Indoor pool; Sauna; Hot tub; Tennis courts; Bicycle rentals; Boat rentals; Fishing rentals; Golf; Playground equipment; Sailing charters; Babysitting (by pre-arrangement); Organized activities for kids

The Resort at Port Ludlow, formerly The Admiralty Resort, is a large and elaborate operation, offering an extensive array of activity options. The management is emphatic about the resort being "family-oriented" and the evidence seems to bear them out. The resort went on a limited-operations schedule for the winter, and was due to resume full operations in the spring. Be sure to call before you go to find out what activities and facilities will be offered when you want to visit.

Rooms at the resort have twin or queen beds and private baths. Apartments have living room, fully equipped kitchen, dining room, fireplace, private deck and view. The units are individually owned and furnished and several families could share one of the larger units with ease—a good way to cut down the cost of a stay at Port Ludlow.

Grounds are large and well-maintained and there's lots of room for children to explore and roam. There are paved bicycle paths, nature hikes and lots of water sports: boating, fishing, clamming and crabbing. A recreation director arranges field games, water games on the lagoon and trips to nearby places like the Olympic Game Farm and Port Townsend.

The Harbormaster is the name of the resort's restaurant. It's expensive. Dinner entrees for adults begin at around $10 and on the children's menu at around $7. A better alternative at the resort is the deli at the golf course, which serves hamburgers, hot dogs and sandwiches. If you feel like traveling for food, The Chimacum Cafe in Chimacum (about ten miles away) is a family restaurant with good food (and lots of it), reasonable prices, but no liquor. An even further trek to Sequim (35 miles) will give you excellent fish dishes at moderate prices at The Three Crabs.

Washington Coast

Many familiar images of the Pacific Northwest are found in this area: soaring mountains and abundant wildlife in the Olympic National Park, rain forests in the Olympic National Forest, miles-long stretches of wide sandy beaches, quaint little towns, Indian-nation reservations with 500-year histories—the Makah, the Ozette, the Quileute, the Hoh and the Quinault.

The area stretches from Neah Bay at the entrance to the Strait of Juan de Fuca, passage to Puget Sound, south to Ilwaco where the Columbia River empties into the Pacific Ocean.

If you want to take in both the beaches and the mountains and rain forests, the most appropriate lodging is at Kalaloch. If the wonderful ocean "out of the cradle endlessly rocking" is your goal, the choices are along the North Beach and at Long Beach. These places are popular holiday and vacation spots for families, and have many natural and man-made attractions.

Here is a closer look at these three areas:

Kalaloch

From Cape Flattery (Neah Bay), northwesternmost point of the continental U.S., south to Kalaloch the ocean beach is either Indian land or national park. Right at Kalaloch are some of the wildest surf and best beachcombing. Logs and glass fish net balls are washed in from distant places. Driftwood is plentiful.

Kalaloch is also a good home base for day trips to explore a rain forest, to follow a three-mile boardwalk from Lake Ozette to remote beaches, and to visit the picturesque Makah Indian village at Neah Bay. The Makah Cultural and Research Center, owned and operated by the Makah Indian Nation, is open every day during summer months and closed Monday and Tuesday from September 16 through May 31. In 1970 tidal erosion exposed a group of 500-year-old Ozette

homes, 15 miles south of Neah Bay, where Makah people had lived
well into the 20th century. Scores of artifacts from the dig are on dis-
play at the Cultural Center. Here and elsewhere in the village carvings, baskets and art work by the Makah are on sale. You probably
will see Makah fishing for salmon as they have done for countless
years. There are numerous places, including the Kalaloch Lodge,
where information is available on rain forest and other park hikes, and
other attractions in the area.

North Beach

Washington's most accessible broad, sandy ocean beaches extend
south of Moclips to Ocean Shores, a stretch of about 20 miles with
numerous turn-offs to the beach and several villages. There is even
beach driving at a sedate 25 miles an hour. Razor clam digging is the
favorite sport, in season. License required. There is always a shore
breeze that makes for super kite flying. Shell collecting and driftwood
gathering are fun on beach walks.

The compactness of the area makes it easy to reach a restaurant,
to shop for groceries, and to take in the numerous attractions at the
Ocean Shores tourist area where there is golf, tennis, horseback riding, bowling and ocean fishing.

Long Beach

The Long Beach Peninsula, about a three-hour drive from Seattle,
comes as close as possible to being a foolproof family getaway destination
regardless of family ages, weather and time of year.

There are nine towns and villages ranging from quiet to lively, and from
a few score residents to 1243 in Long Beach, the largest. Stretching 29
miles from Ledbetter Point to the Columbia River, the peninsula claims
the longest (29 miles) drivable ocean beach in the world.

The area is loaded with history. Turn-of-the century houses abound.
Oysterville, founded about 1854 to harvest the Willapa Harbor oysterbeds,
supplied San Francisco restaurants during gold rush days. Nearby Nahcotta is now the oyster center. A narrow-gauge railroad completed in 1889
met steamers and ferries. One surviving depot is now a tavern. Fort
Columbia, built in 1899 as part of a Columbia River and coast fortification
system, is now a museum. Lewis and Clark camped near the fort November 15-25, 1905 and got their first view of the Pacific. An estimated 230
ships have been wrecked at or near the entrance to the Columbia River,
called the most dangerous waters in the world.

All of this provides a colorful background for today's visitors. The broad, sandy, flat beach has clam digging in season. Beach walking means looking at old shipwrecks, hunting glass fish net balls from far-off places; collecting shells; digging in the sand and reveling in the ocean air.

While summer months offer more opportunities, there are plenty of things to do year-round. Long Beach and Seaview have numerous shops and galleries, an unusual and sometimes bizarre gift shop and curio museum, amusement arcades and go-carts, and eating places ranging from expensive gourmet to snacks. There are two nine-hole golf courses.

Nearby are the largest rhododendron nursery in the world and a research center for the local cranberry industry started early this century with vines from Cape Cod. At the north tip of the peninsula the Ledbetter Point State Park has pine forests, salt marshes and sand dunes. It includes part of the Willapa Wildlife Refuge attracting thousands of birds. Access is open to the public except for a certain area that is closed from April through August to protect the nesting of snowy plovers, a small shorebird with a declining population.

At the south end of the peninsula are Fort Columbia, the old fishing village of Ilwaco, the Cape Disappointment lighthouse, oldest operating lighthouse in the Pacific Northwest, the North Head lighthouse and Fort Canby State Park. Before electricity the Cape Disappointment light, first lit in 1856, burned five gallons of oil per night through five wicks, each 18 inches across. The Cape Disappointment Coast Guard Station is close to the mouth of the Columbia where the bar between the river and the ocean creates treacherous water conditions that have wrecked hundreds of ships. The Coast Guard station conducts a one-of-its-kind boat-handlers school that draws people from throughout the country. Under the right conditions visitors to the north jetty in Fort Canby State Park can watch Coast Guardsmen launch boats through the heavy surf to practice rescue missions.

A quick trip to Oregon is also easy across the 4.1-mile toll bridge from Megler, a few miles east of Ilwaco, to Astoria, Oregon, across the mighty Columbia River.

HOW TO GET THERE

From Seattle take I-5 to just south of Olympia, turn west on U.S. 101 and after a few miles turn west on Highway 8 toward Aberdeen. The road later becomes Highway 12. If your destination is the Long Beach area turn south on Highway 101 near Aberdeen toward Raymond. If you are heading for the North Beach or Kalaloch areas, follow Highway 109 through Aberdeen and Hoquiam to the ocean beaches. The roads are well posted.

To make the Olympic Peninsula Loop counter-clockwise from Seattle, take either the Winslow ferry from downtown Seattle or the Kingston ferry

from Edmonds, Exit 177 on I-5 north of Seattle. On either route follow
the signs to Port Gamble and the Hood Canal Floating Bridge on Highway
104. Follow Highway 104 as it joins U.S. 101 to Port Angeles. If you plan
to visit Neah Bay on the Makah Indian Reservation take Highway 112 just
west of Port Angeles. If your destination is Kalaloch and the ocean
beaches, stay on U.S. 101. Because there is no tourist lodging at Neah
Bay, many visitors travel there on a side trip from Kalaloch, Lake
Quinault or Port Angeles. Neah Bay is 70 miles from Port Angeles, and
about 100 miles from Kalaloch. Seattle to Kalaloch through Port Angeles
is 180 miles.
From Portland take U.S. 30 north along the Columbia River to Astoria.
Take the toll bridge across the Columbia from Astoria to Megler. Follow
U.S. 101 to Highway 102 for Long Beach places, or continue on U.S. 101
to Aberdeen-Hoquiam to connect with Highway 103 to North Beaches.
    If your destination for a short holiday is the North Beach area the quick-
est route from Seattle is about 140 miles via Olympia and Aberdeen.
From Portland, through Astoria, it is about 115 miles to the Long Beach
area.

WHAT TO SEE ON THE WAY
    A stop at Olympia, 60 miles south of Seattle on I-5, to see the state
capitol building, the capitol campus and some of the state buildings is interesting, especially if the legislature is in session. Regular annual sessions
start in January and usually run to June. The capitol is modeled on the national capitol in Washington, D.C., and contains the offices of the governor, secretary of state, state treasurer and state auditor as well as the
legislative chambers. The chambers of the state supreme court and the
state library are worth seeing. Downstairs in the library is an excellent
historical mural by Kenneth Callahan, a leading Washington artist who
lives on the Long Beach peninsula.
    Traveling between Olympia and Aberdeen watch for the controversial
mothballed nuclear power plants of the Washington Public Power Supply
System between Elma and Satsop. The cooling towers are huge.
    If you would like to fit a half-day tour of a logging and reforestation
operation into your trip telephone in advance to Carolyn Luark at
Boise Cascade Corporation in Aberdeen at (206)532-7331. Children
should be at least seven.

Kalaloch Lodge

Star Route 1, Box 1100, Kalaloch, WA 98331
206-962-2271
Moderate—$38-$50 for lodge rooms; $66 for log cabins; $58-$78 for
scenic bluff cabins; $3 per extra person
MC, V

Directions: Located 70 miles north of Hoquiam on U.S. 101.

At A Glance: Cribs; Kitchens; Restaurant; Pets OK.

Kalaloch offers hotel, motel and cabin accommodations. The lodge rooms are reported to be a bit noisy. The newest facilities are the log cabins, but they have no ocean view. The older cabins are perched on a high bluff overlooking the ocean and have lovely views. Cabins are equipped with small kitchenettes, but you must bring your own utensils, pots, and food. There is a small grocery store on site.

Though the resort is perched above the beach, the trail down is easy to negotiate. The beach is beautiful—filled with driftwood and fun to comb, but the water is too cold and too dangerous for small children. Luckily there's a small quiet lagoon for paddling, located right in front of the lodge, and you can find protected coves further north that are safe for swimming.

There are two restaurants in the lodge—the Kalaloch Dining Room, and the Kalaloch Coffee Shop, both of which have the same menu and prices (expensive). The first is quite elegant. If you take the children, go early. High chairs are available and the service is good. The Coffee Shop has no view but, more important, has plastic benches and formica tables, as well as a counter for faster service.

Comments

"Our daughter had a sleeping space which was separated from the main part of the cabin by a folding door—we liked that a lot."

"You might run out of things to do if the weather was bad because there's no pool."

The Beachwood Resort

Box 116, Copalis Beach, WA 98535
206-289-2177
Inexpensive—$45 for 2 in beachfront units; $39 for 2 in side units with
no direct ocean view; $4 per extra person
No credit cards

Directions: From Aberdeen, take Hwy 109 to Ocean Beaches. This
North Beach resort is located between Ocean City and Copalis on
Hwy 109.

At A Glance: Cribs; Kitchens; TV in 8 oceanfront units (TV cable
plug if you bring your own); Indoor pool (seasonal); Sauna; Indoor
recreation room with ping pong, barbecue; Deck tennis and lawn
games; Playground.

Beachwood is an old ocean beach resort with a good reputation for
friendliness to families. It's small—only 21 units—and is located right
on the beach, which is long and wide. Each cabin has a kitchen, a
separate bedroom with two double beds, a living room with a hide-a-
bed and a fireplace (lots of wood provided). Furnishings are worn but
very clean.

The covered heated swimming pool is only open seasonally—be sure
to ask, as it provides good entertainment when it's raining. The
playground is fenced and has swings and a slide. Small campfires are
permitted in the dunes bordering the beach, and clam digging season
is one of the best times to visit the resort.

Comments

"A very safe environment for children. Great place for kite flying,
walking, running, sand dollars, fresh ocean breezes. Kids can tear
around without bothering anyone."

Iron Springs Resort

Copalis Beach, WA 98535
206-276-4230
*Moderate—$70 for a large, 2-family cabin; rates vary according to size
of cabin and number of people*
MC, V

Directions: From Aberdeen, take Hwy 109 to Ocean Beaches. Iron Springs is located between Copalis Beach and Pacific Beach on Hwy 109.

At A Glance: Cribs ($4 for entire stay); Kitchens; Indoor pool; Pets OK.

The ocean views are spectacular from Iron Springs' cabins, both on sunny summer days and stormy winter ones. Cabins are fairly secluded so there's a real sense of privacy, and the rather eclectic interiors are comfortable and durable. Kitchens are fully equipped, and each cabin has a fireplace. Some of the cabins are located on a high bluff overlooking the ocean; the path to the beach has steep stairs, and the best access to the south part of the beach when the tide is high is along the road.

Activity centers around the beach, which is perfect for building sandcastles or razor clam digging during the day and for campfires at night. Tide tables are available in the office. Although there is no restaurant at the resort, cinnamon rolls and chowder are available at the office.

Comments

"We like Iron Springs because the cabins are a little funky and because we don't have to worry at all about the boys' behavior."

"Kids are tolerated and encouraged!"

The Sandpiper Beach Resort

P.O. Box A, Pacific Beach, WA 98571
206-276-4580
Moderate—$37-$62 for 2; some units sleep up to 6 people ($98-$135);
$6 per extra person over 14 years old, $3 under 14
MC, V

Directions: From Aberdeen take Hwy 109 to Ocean Beaches. Located 6 miles north of Copalis Beach on Hwy 109.

At A Glance: Cribs; Kitchens; Playground; Pets OK ($5 per night)

The Sandpiper is a perfect place to go for a hassle-free, leisurely and low-key getaway from the city. The 29 units are of various configurations—studios, suites, separate cabins—and all have complete housekeeping facilities. All but one of the 29 units have full ocean views and all but three have fireplaces. The units above the first floor have full lanais with room for barbecues, hanging out wet clothes and displaying "treasures." Each unit is equipped with puzzles, magazines and rocking chairs for parents with infants. The grounds are beautifully landscaped and maintained.

Activities at the Sandpiper clearly center around the beach, although even in the summer it can be chilly and windy. There are strong currents and thus no real swimming for kids. Volleyballs can be borrowed from the office, and there's an on -the-beach playground with slide, big tires and a see-saw. A well-stocked gift shop has lots of books, toys and kites for children. An outside firepit is a great place for barbecues and fireworks.

During the summer, the Sandpiper is almost exclusively a family resort with kids of all ages around. Many families book the same week year after year, so early reservations are definitely advised.

There are many small restaurants in Ocean Shores, 15 miles south. A bit closer, four miles away in Moclips, is the Ocean Crest Resort & Dinner House, located on Highway 109. The restaurant provides high chairs and is tolerant of kids. Breakfast and lunch menus are good and basic; dinner is Continental and American style. Dinner entrees for adults are $8-$17, and children's portions are $5.

Comments

"The Sandpiper is extremely well-managed by the resident owners and one other manager. They remember you from year to year. If anything is amiss in your unit it is immediately taken care of."

"Miles of unspoiled beaches full of sand dollars, shells, sea stars and driftwood."

Klipsan Beach Cottages

Ocean Park, WA 98640
206-665-4888
Inexpensive—$40 for 1-bedroom cabin; $52 for 2-bedroom cabin
MC, V

Directions: To reach the Long Beach area, take Hwy 101 South from Hwy 12, east of Aberdeen, go through Raymond to Seaview, then go north on Hwy 103 to Klipsan Beach.

At A Glance: Kitchens; TV (in some cabins)

There are a total of eight Klipsan Beach Cottages—comfortable cedar shingle cabins with fireplaces and west-facing decks. The expanse of dunes and sea visible from the cabins helps make up for the fact that they are very close together. Cabins have either one or two bedrooms, a hide-a-bed in the living room, and fully equipped kitchens. You must bring your own linens or pay $4 per night.

There are usually lots of children around—the place is a popular one for families. An added attraction for those who like to play hide-and-seek is a small rhododendron forest and a safe stretch of dunes between the cabins and the beach.

If you want to travel ten miles for an expensive meal in an elegant place, try the Shelburne Inn in Seaview. Though this is clearly an adult restaurant, our source says: "Our kids were greeted with equanimity and immediately provided with a drawing of the stained glass window to color along with sharp, unbroken crayons in a porcelain mug. There is also a gift shop for older kids to poke around after the meal." In nearby Nahcotta, The Ark, with its less fragile interior, exceptional cuisine and relaxed atmosphere, is a good bet for families. A favorite spot of the late gastronome, James Beard, it has a separate children's menu and is located at the water's edge near the oyster works. Another safe choice for a meal out is My Mom's Pie Kitchen, located in Long Beach at Pacific Highway 103 and 12th S., about seven miles south of Klipsan Beach: pies are excellent, and they serve a few other things like chili dogs, quiches, clam chowder and shrimp salad.

Comments

"The style is inoffensive, if not elegant, and there's nothing your kids can destroy."

"Wood was provided for the fireplace but it was very wet!"

The Sou'Wester Lodge

Beach Access Rd. (38th Pl.), P.O. Box 102, Seaview, WA 98644
206-642-2542
Inexpensive—From $34 for 2; $3 additional per child
MC, V

Directions: From Hwy 12 east of Aberdeen, take U.S. 101 south to
Long Beach to Hwy 103; go south 2 blocks to 38th Pl.; turn right
towards the beach.

At A Glance: Cribs; Kitchens; TV (requires reservation); Pets OK;
Babysitting (by pre-arrangement)

    The Sou'Wester, originally "Westborough House" when built in
1892 by a U.S. senator from Oregon, is now in the competent hands
of Len and Miriam Atkins. Apartments (minimum stay one month) and
rooms in the main lodge are supplemented by four beach cabins.
Cabins have no fireplaces but do have kitchens and lots of clean
towels. Everything is weathered, inside and out, and decor is
described by the owners as "early Salvation Army." The Atkinses
"want to attract the kind of people who will come in spite of the fact
that the place is not painted or furnished like the Hilton—people who
are looking for a place where the setting itself is meaningful." Located on three acres of land, Sou'wester Lodge also offers camping
sites, RV hook-ups, hot showers and laundry facilities.
    An interesting sideline is that the Atkinses offer "Oceanside
Retreats for Parents." These workshops are both for groups and for
individuals (the latter set up by appointment). The Atkinses' involve-
ment in education spans decades: they left South Africa in 1951 to
study A.S. Neill's methods of children's self-government in England.
From 1951 to 1966 they worked in Israel, where Len was Co-
Director of "Neve Zeilim," the Residential Therapy Facility for the
treatment of emotionally disturbed kibbutz children. While there, he
was invited by Bruno Bettelheim to join the faculty of the University
of Chicago Orthogenic School.
    There are a couple of suggestions for restaurants in the area. The
Barge in Raymond (Highway 101) makes a good stop on your way to
Seaview and has pizza and terrific burgers. Closer to the Sou'Wester
are Chico's Pizza in Long Beach, about a mile north of the resort,
and the Harbor Hut in Ilwaco, three miles away. Chico's is sort of a
local hangout but serves good pizza, has good service and provides
high chairs. Harbor Hut has good general food—club sandwiches to
fresh seafood specials—and it's fresh and hot. The restaurant is located

on a spit in the harbor and you can watch fishing boats come in
and out.

Comments

"The drawing card is the people—they are *wonderful*—and were
great to the kids."

"There is a beach access road near the cabins which made me ner-
vous. The local teen population uses it a lot. Also cars can drive on
the beach so I never felt comfortable with the kids at the beach
alone."

"We thought it was a good value."

The Sou'Wester Lodge

Mount Rainier

At 14,410 feet Mt. Rainier dominates the Seattle-Tacoma skyline. This great ice cream cone in the sky does not make an appearance every day, but when it does the experience is awesome to the beholder. The closer the view, the greater the thrill. Fortunately, you can get close enough to touch the majestic peak without getting into mountain climbing.

This is an area that has year-round attractions. Two of our recommended places are just outside Mount Rainier National Park. Ashford offers winter sports and casual snow enjoyment. There are complete downhill skiing facilities at the White Pass ski area.

Most visitors pay homage to the magic mountain during the spring, summer and fall months. The glaciers and snowfields are still in evidence then. The alpine meadows above timberline (about 6000 feet) offer trail walking that suits every age. Colored masses of alpine flowers begin to bloom about mid-June, depending on weather, and reach their peak in late July or early August.

Park facilities include rustic lodges and visitor centers. The latter have exhibits, visual programs and lectures that add much to appreciation and enjoyment of the park. You receive full information when you enter the park.

HOW TO GET THERE

Take I-5 south from Seattle to Exit 142 to Puyallup on Highway 161. At Eatonville take Highway 7 to Elbe. Or from the Tacoma area take I-5 Exit 127 to Highway 512 to connect with Highway 7 to Elbe. At Elbe take Highway 706 to Ashford and Paradise Inn, or continue on Highway 7 and turn east on Highway 12 to White Pass.

WHAT TO SEE ON THE WAY

Northwest Trek, a wildlife park, is six miles north of Eatonville on Highway 161, about 55 miles from Seattle. The park, owned and operated by the Metropolitan Park District of Tacoma, opens daily at 10 a.m. from mid-February through October with weekend and special holiday openings the rest of the year. There are a picnic area, rest-rooms, snack bar and covered outdoor eating area. A variety of North American wild animals are seen on an hour-long tram ride. There are also foot trails. Call the park at (206)832-6116, or call 325-5566 in Seattle for a recorded message.

Also near Eatonville is Pioneer Farm, a hands-on living portrayal of frontier life with costumed guides. By reservation only; (206)832-6300.

At Elbe from May through September a vintage steam train offers two-hour rides through scenic mountain valleys with entertainment at the end of the ride. A fun trip.

Five miles from Ashford is Moore Family Mountain Crafts located in picturesque log cabins. Visitors may watch and talk with craftsmen such as stained-glass blowers, wood carvers, leather workers, and painters. Merry-go-round rides for 50 cents. In the same area Indian Henri's Wagon Rides offer a 20-minute mountain road trip for $1.50 and a one-hour ride for about $6.50 which includes a meal, songs around a campfire and the story of the Legend of Indian Henri. A real thrill for kids.

Gateway Inn

Ashford, WA 98304
206-569-2506
Inexpensive—$34.50 per night
AE, MC, V

Directions: Located at the southwest corner of the entrance to Mt. Rainier National Park.

At A Glance: Cribs; Restaurant; Babysitting (by pre-arrangement); Pets OK

The appeal of the Gateway Inn is the opportunity to enjoy the natural beauty of Mt. Rainier National Park. In the summer, hiking opportunities in the area are endless. From November to March, snow at the Inn's level allows for safe sledding on the premises and skiing at Paradise on cross-country trails.

The cabins, with fireplaces and heating, are made for young families: warm and safe, they're rustic enough to allow Mom and Dad to relax, and kids love the feeling of staying in their own little log house.

The Gateway Inn has a restaurant and coffee shop which offer inexpensive to moderately priced meals. In addition, there are three other eating options. The Growly Bear Family Bakery, located 1¼ miles before the entrance to Mt. Rainier, has scrumptious home baked bread and pastries, and a cute bear motif. Kids can watch the baking in progress. The Copper Kettle, located three miles before the Mt. Rainier entrance (a popular way of measuring distances in this neck of the woods), has a moderately priced menu with specials for children. Its small, informal mountain lodge atmosphere and cheerful college student employees make children feel special. Home baked bread, fresh trout, and wild blackberry pie are delicious. Open seven days a week from April to October, weekends only November to March. If your children are old enough to behave in a fancier setting, you might consider Alexander's, a restaurant offering fine dining, a moderate to expensive menu, and housed in a large wooden castle-like structure two miles from the entrance to Mt. Rainier.

Comments

"A stay at the Gateway Inn offers no drawbacks for a family seeking a safe and rustic overnight."

Paradise Inn

Paradise, WA 98398/Mt. Rainier Guest Services, Star Route, Ashford,
WA 98304
206-569-2291/Reservations: 206-569-2275
Inexpensive—$28 for a room with shared bath; $48 for room with bath;
$64 for a 2-room unit with bath; $5 per extra person
MC, V

Directions: Take Hwy 7 south at Elbe, pick up Rt 706, head east to
Paradise.

At A Glance: Cribs; Restaurant; Hiking trails; Skiing trails; Ski lessons & rentals

Paradise Inn was first opened in 1917 and has the feel of all such
national park edifices, including the massive lobby with huge open
beams and big stone fireplaces at either end. This is a busy place during the day, as there are lots of daytime tourists. Accommodations
are comfortable but in no way roomy or deluxe. A few board games
can be checked out from the desk and there's a gift shop if you need
to buy a coloring book, but most entertainment is centered outdoors,
where walking and hiking opportunities are limitless. Guided nature
walks for all ages, ranging in length from ½ hour to three hours, are
offered during the day and at night there are slide shows on nature
and geology in the lobby at 9 p.m., as well as an occasional movie.

The Visitors' Center, within walking distance of the Inn, has lots of
exhibits and movies about the mountain, and Longmire, 13 miles down
the road, has a small climbing museum. The National Park Inn at
Longmire is the Park's center for winter operations, and if you want
to stay on the mountain, rent skis or take lessons, that's the place to
go. Cross-country trails are available up the hill at Paradise, but Paradise Inn is open only from early June to early October.

There are a number of options for eating when you stay at Paradise. The dining room offers a children's menu with $4 entrees, but
adult dinners are expensive ($10). Kid tolerance is high, service is
good, and booster chairs and high chairs are available. Off the lobby
there's a cash-only snack bar with a very limited menu—hot choco-
late, hot dogs, potato chips—and no place to sit. The Visitors' Center
also has a snack bar with a wider range of food, but it doesn't open
until 10 a.m. and it closes at 6 p.m. on weekdays and 7 p.m. on
weekends. Longmire's combination cafeteria/dining room is casual, but
it's 13 miles down the road from Paradise. If you *are* willing to drive,
some of the restaurants outside the entrance to the park in Ashford

probably give you your best value. For specifics, see restaurants listed under Gateway Inn above.

Comments

"Be sure to check the weather. One June we took a nephew who
was visiting from the east coast to Paradise so we could show him the
mountains of the west and he couldn't see a thing through the
blizzard."

"Rangers are quite helpful in choosing hikes to suit the family
group."

"It was especially nice to have the Visitors' Center open after dinner when time could have been heavy on our hands."

The Village Inn

White Pass, WA 98937
Dial Operator and ask for toll station White Pass No. 2
Moderate—Ski season rates: $50 for economy units (2-4 people); $70 for standard units (4-6 people); $90 for deluxe units (8 people); special mid-week rates on lodging, lift tickets and lessons (2-night minimum); special summer rates.
MC, V

Directions: On Hwy 7 at Elbe take turnoff for Morton. Head east on Rt 12 until you reach White Pass.

At A Glance: Kitchens; Restaurant; Outdoor pool; Hiking; Skiing

The Village Inn is a group of individually owned condominiums. All have a kitchenette and bath, and some have fireplaces. Bed linens and towels are provided. Economy units have either a double bed or a double bed and bunks or hide-a-bed. Standard units are either 1) a studio with a loft, having double bed or hide-a-bed below with bunks or single beds in the loft, or 2) one-bedroom units with a living room with a double hide-a-bed and a bedroom with a double bed and bunks. The four deluxe units have one bedroom and are in high demand. All units have a ski storage shed, and most have a nice view of the ski slopes and mountains.

The emphasis here is obviously on skiing. The resort facilities include four double chairs, a rope tow, ski rentals and repair shop and 15 kilometers of maintained cross-country trails which go around a small lake. The outdoor swimming pool is heated in winter.

A good place to stop for food on the way to White Pass is The Wagon Wheel in Morton, a diner that serves good, cheap hamburgers. Once at the resort, there's a cafeteria at the Daylodge, and a restaurant with moderate prices that's probably best for kids seven and older. If you're cooking your own, there's a grocery store on site.

Comments
"Good value for the price."

"It's great fun to run through the snow to jump into the pool!"

CENTRAL
& EASTERN
WASHINGTON

Central
Washington

If the purpose of your holiday is a shift of scenery and a drastic change in climate, a drive over the Cascades into central Washington will achieve your goal. Although the three recommended places can be covered on a map by a 50-cent coin, they vary in scenery. Leavenworth is close to the east slope of the Cascades. Cle Elum is a little beyond the foothills and Ellensburg is down in Kittitas Valley, farther from the mountains, drier and sunnier.

Leavenworth is a delightful town done up in Bavarian style. Although it is an enjoyable area at all seasons of the year, it literally blooms in summer and fall when festivities are in full swing. The colorful show of autumn foliage from Stevens Pass down the canyon to Leavenworth attracts many visitors.

Cle Elum provides a good taste of the old west of cattle ranching and horses. It is genuine. The ranches, mountains and streams have been around a long time.

Ellensburg is a cowboy town. The highway passes Stuart Anderson's famous ranch where beef originates for many of his well-known restaurants. The big event of the year is the Ellensburg Rodeo, always held on Labor Day weekend. It is one of the big-league rodeos on a par in the Pacific Northwest with the noted Pendleton, Oregon, Roundup. The Indian encampment at Ellensburg by the Yakima Indians has been an outstanding feature for years. It provides a unique opportunity to see traditional Indian camp activities at close range.

HOW TO GET THERE

The direct route to Leavenworth is over Stevens Pass on U.S. 2: Take I-5 north 27 miles from Seattle to Exit 194 at Everett to get on U.S. 2, or take Highway 405 on the east side of Lake Washington to connect with Highway 522 near Bothell. Follow Highway 522 to junction with U.S. 2 at Monroe. Signs read Monroe-Wenatchee. There is a new access to Highway 405 and Highway 522 at Exit 182 on I-5 ten miles north of Seattle. Leavenworth is also an easy drive via Highway

I-90 over Snoqualmie Pass. Turn off I-90 at Exit 85 near Cle Elum on
Highway 970 which shortly becomes U.S. 97 through Blewett Pass,
connecting with Highway 2 just south of Leavenworth.

To reach Cle Elum and Ellensburg take I-90 from Seattle through
Snoqualmie Pass. From Seattle, Cle Elum is about 90 miles and
Ellensburg about 110.

From Portland take I-84 east along the Columbia River to U.S. 97
at Biggs. Cross the Columbia and follow U.S. 97 through Goldendale,
Yakima and Ellensburg to Cle Elum. Cle Elum is 235 miles from
Portland.

WHAT TO SEE ON THE WAY

Both Stevens Pass and Snoqualmie Pass summit areas are popular
skiing developments with complete facilities. At other times of the
year both areas are good rest stops with trail walks, restrooms and
food service. Both routes offer spectacular river scenery and good
fishing and rafting in season. Leavenworth is at the head of the
Wenatchee River valley and also has an enchanting stream called Icicle
River, warm enough for swimming despite its name. Cle Elum and
Ellensburg share the Yakima River for fishing and boating.

Near Cle Elum is the old coal mining town of Roslyn. Although the
mines are inactive the town lives on with many lived-in "museums"
and historians of the old days. This is the gateway to the Salmon le
Sac and Lake Cle Elum recreation areas.

Beyond Ellensburg about 20 miles is the Gingko Petrified Forest
Museum. The museum is on a bluff overlooking the Columbia River
and has unusual exhibits that explain this geologically rich area. What
looks like a vast expanse of water and bluffs becomes as exciting as a
futuristic space movie set.

Brown's Farm

11150 Hwy 209, Leavenworth, WA 98826
509-548-7863
Moderate—$40-$45; $6 per child (under 4 years free)
No credit cards

Directions: In Leavenworth, take Hwy 209 north 1½ miles to Brown's Farm.

At A Glance: Cribs; Breakfast; Farm animals; Babysitting (by pre-arrangement)

The Browns—Steve, Wendi and their three kids—bill their farm as "A Bed & Breakfast Home Place." The big house is made of hand hewn logs and rocks from the Icicle River Valley, and has a huge wrap-around porch. Two of the six bedrooms are used for guests; children should bring a sleeping bag. Since Leavenworth festivals are crowded, it's best to reserve at least six months in advance (minimum stay two nights during festival weekends) for the Mai Fest, Autumn Leaf Festival, and the Christmas Lighting.

Brown's Farm has a dog, a pony, a horse, a goat, sheep, five rabbits and a rooster with a full henhouse. Children can gather eggs in the afternoons. In the summer there's swimming at a nearby swimming hole on the Icicle River or at the large outdoor public pool in Leavenworth. In the winter kids can sled right down the side of the

Brown's Farm

mountain at the farm. Snowshoeing, sleigh rides and cross-country skiing are great in the area—there's a lighted course for nighttime, and the Browns will help arrange ski rentals.

Breakfast consists of French toast, eggs, whole wheat pancakes, homemade jams and jellies, orange juice and coffee. Omelettes are a specialty. You can watch hummingbirds, and sometimes deer, from the breakfast table. There are numerous casual restaurants in Leavenworth, an easy bike ride away.

Comments

"Mr. Brown's breakfast cooking is outstanding. The family atmosphere is genuine and warm. There is no TV or radio—just lots of animals and kids."

Hidden Valley Ranch

Route 2, Box 111, Cle Elum, WA 98922
509-674-2422
Expensive—$44-$54 per person for partial plan; $70-$80 per person for full-service plan; $100 for housekeeping unit for 4; extra charges for extra people in cabins; children under 4 years free
No credit cards

Directions: Take I-90 to Exit 85. Turn off and follow SR 970 (Blewett Pass Hwy) for 8 miles. Take a right on Hidden Valley Rd. and follow it for 3 miles to the ranch.

At A Glance: Kitchens; Entertainment center (books, piano, pool table); Outdoor pool; Horseback riding; Hiking trails; Lawn games; Skiing trails; Fishing; Babysitting (by pre-arrangement)

Hidden Valley Ranch is quite a spread—800 acres of ranch, field, river and gently rolling hills. It's an operating horse ranch—they breed, break and train the 30 horses, and farm to support them. Riding is the emphasis of any vacation at Hidden Valley Ranch, where there are two or three trail rides a day, and the temperaments of the horses are varied enough to appeal to any level of rider.

Cabins are charming and rustic but have electric heat and showers. Several are equipped with kitchenettes. Housekeeping units at $100 a night accommodate four to six people. Riding, meals in the main lodge, and other activities are charged separately. If you choose this option, try to bring your food with you, as the nearest shopping area is in Cle Elum, 12 miles distant. Should you choose the full-service plan (standard cabin $70 per person per day, or deluxe cabin $80), rates include meals, lodging, and two rides daily, as well as all other activities such as trail breakfasts, cookouts, hayrides, playdays and rodeo events as they occur. The partial plan rates of $44 for the standard cabin and $54 for the deluxe include meals but not rides and activities. There's a minimum stay of two days, and guests who stay for one or more weeks are entitled to one free day per week. A 15 per cent gratuity is added to all bills, so no other tipping is necessary. In the winter, the ranch has Nordic skiing weekends with skiing on the fields, meadows and trails of the ranch or nearby Blewett Pass.

Comments

"Our six-year-old rode for the first time and loved it!"

"The great managers, Terry and Mike, go out of their way to make you comfortable. Meals are delicious—large, home cooked, buffet, and all you can eat."

"After dark we had star-filled chats around the outdoor fireplace with other guests."

Holidome (Holiday Inn)

I-90 and U.S. 97, Ellensburg, WA 98926
509-925-9801
Moderate—$44-$48; children under 17 free; rollaways $5
AE, CB, DC, MC, V

Directions: I-90 west to U.S. 97 north. The hotel is located at the intersection of these two major routes.

At A Glance: Cribs; TV; Restaurant; Indoor pool; Play area; Pets OK

Although a Holiday Inn might strike you as a strange choice for this book, we've chosen this one for its generic value. Not all Holiday Inns are Holidomes, but there are enough of them scattered around the country that it's worth knowing about the concept. A Holidome is essentially an enclosed entertainment area attached to the rest of the hotel complex. In Ellensburg, the Holidome features a heated pool, a game area and video games. Other Holidomes, such as the one located in Everett, offer additional features like sauna, waterfall, theater and lecture room. Others have hot tubs, coffee and gift shops, putting green and racquetball.

A restaurant to try in Ellensburg is McCullough's, which serves good food at moderate prices. Decor is like an old-fashioned parlor and kids are well tolerated.

Comments

"The room was clean and comfortable, nothing spectacular but adequate. The extras are what make this place special."

Lake Chelan

This area offers some of the most spectacular scenery in the state combined with recreational opportunities ranging from isolated wilderness to the comfortable pleasures of a small lakefront town. The narrow 55-mile-long lake, 1500 feet deep in some places, is fed by 27 glaciers and 59 streams. The constant sun in summer warms it at the south end for good swimming, windsurfing and water skiing. The deep, cold, icy blue water in the north part runs about 55° even in July.

It's not just chamber of commerce talk that established Lake Chelan as "a place in the sun." Whatever the summer weather may be west of the Cascades, it is a good bet that the four-hour drive to Lake Chelan will produce warm, cloudless, sunny skies.

The town of Chelan at the south end has a permanent population of around 3000. There are a hospital, 18-hole golf course, and many restaurants and stores that have learned to adapt to seasonal volumes of visitors. The city park has good playground equipment. Bumper boats can be rented. Nine miles north on Highway 150 along the lake is the non-incorporated village of Manson, a resort area as well as the center of a prosperous apple industry.

At the head of the lake is the isolated community of Stehekin, accessible only by boat or plane. Although isolated, this beautiful area draws some 40,000 people a year who are interested in one or more of the following activities: hiking, camping, backpacking, mountain climbing, boating, canoeing, rafting, guided horseback trips, bicycle and moped trails, fishing and just plain relaxing in the sun. There isn't a single telephone. The National Park Service maintains a district office here. The lectures, like those in any national park or recreation area, add much to enjoyment of the place. The ranger leads nature walks.

HOW TO GET THERE

From the Seattle area there are two main routes with about equal travel time of three to four hours.

One route goes through Stevens Pass. Take I-5 27 miles north
from Seattle to Exit 194 to U.S. 2. Near Wenatchee turn north on
U.S. 97. Or take Highway 405 on the east side of Lake Washington
to connect with Highway 522 near Bothell. Follow 522 to junction
with U.S. 2 at Monroe. There is a new access route to Highway 405
and Highway 522 at Exit 182 on I-5, ten miles north of Seattle.

The other route goes through Snoqualmie Pass. Take I-90 from
Seattle to Exit 85 near Cle Elum. Follow Highway 970 merging with
U.S. 97 in a few miles through Blewett Pass to connect with Highway
2. Turn north on U.S. 97 near Wenatchee.

From Portland take I-84 east along the Columbia River to U.S. 97
at Biggs. Cross the Columbia and follow U.S. 97 north through Goldendale, Yakima and Ellensburg through Blewett Pass to U.S. 2 and
Wenatchee. Follow U.S. 97 north from Wenatchee along the Columbia
to Highway 150 to Chelan.

WHAT TO SEE ON THE WAY

The Stevens Pass route is scenic and passes through Skykomish
River towns dating from gold mining days. Although the Stevens Pass
summit area is known mainly for skiing, it is a pleasant rest stop in
any season. On the east side of the Cascades the Bavarian-style town
of Leavenworth has quaint shops and European-type festivals.

The Snoqualmie Pass route also has good facilities and pleasant surroundings at the summit. The Blewett Pass area has some interesting
roadside places related to gold mining days.

The two routes join just west of Cashmere. This spic-and-span early American town celebrates apples and pioneers. A popular stop is
the Aplet and Cotlet Candy Kitchen where a fruit and nut confection
has been made for 60 years. Visitors are welcome and the kids like
the samples. The Wenatchee River flows down this valley and offers
rafting, boating and fishing.

After you leave Highway 2 and turn north on Highway 97 there are
two special attractions. The Ohme Gardens, open from April through
October, were developed on a high rocky bluff overlooking the Columbia River and the Wenatchee Valley. It took 50 years by a dedicated
family to build this alpine-style garden, rated as one of the outstanding
gardens in the country. Close by on U.S. 97 is Rocky Reach Dam
where you can look a salmon in the eye. The fish ladder viewing
room is where you can observe at close range the salmon swimming
upstream to return to their spawning grounds. There is also a good
geology exhibit and the story of electricity with hands-on gadgets for
kids to operate. Outside the main building is an attractive picnic area.

Campbell's Lodge

P.O. Box 278, Chelan, WA 98816
509-682-2561
Moderate to Expensive—$34-$125, depending on time of year; weekly rates
AE, MC, V

Directions: Located in the center of Chelan on U.S. 97.

At A Glance: Cribs ($5); Kitchens; TV; Restaurant; Outdoor pools (2); Hot tub; Babysitting (by pre-arrangement)

Campbell's is a Chelan institution, having been established in 1901. Since then it has expanded and sprawled, most recently with the acquisition of neighboring Cannons Resort. Units vary from waterfront view units to cottages (on or off the beach) with kitchens, to housekeeping units. Some units accommodate up to six people. Prices are highest in July and August, when a one-bed waterfront unit begins at $66, and the penthouse with two bedrooms, two bathrooms and a fireplace costs $148 a night. Reservations for peak months should be made at least six months in advance, so popular is this place. Rates drop during off-season, with prices being the lowest November to May. A good location is important: request ground floor rooms near the lake if possible.

The outdoor pools are heated, and since the lake is cold well into the summer, this is a plus. There is a sandy beach, so be sure to bring buckets and shovels. There's quite a bit of lawn space for running around.

The restaurant at Campbell's has a children's menu, high chairs, boosters and moderate prices. Children are well tolerated. For pizza suggestions see the listing under Kelly's Resort in this book.

Comments

"There was a crib but it was too small for our two-year-old."

"I thought the accommodation was good for the price."

"It's located at the town's main intersection, so an inquisitive child might wander out—even from a top floor. Small children should be watched."

Pat & Jim Hammett's Mountain Cabin

P.O.Box 72, Stehekin, WA 98852
No Phone—reservations by mail
Inexpensive to Moderate—Cabin sleeps six: $30 in winter; $50 in summer plus cost of boat ($17 round trip for adults, $8.50 for kids); or plane ($21 each passenger each way) from Chelan
No credit cards

Directions: From Chelan, take "Lady of the Lake" boat or Chelan Airways, Inc. charter plane. The Hammetts will meet you at Stehekin Landing and drive you to the cabin.

At A Glance: Crib; Kitchen; Pets OK (Oct. 15—May 15); Babysitting (may be possible); Car

When the Hammetts meet you at the landing, they'll drive you to the spare cabin on their place and acquaint you with the valley on the way home. Once there, you'll find a bedroom with a double bed, an open loft with two twins and a queen-sized hide-a-bed in the living room. There's a limit of six people. The cabin is completely furnished and equipped for housekeeping, with electricity, water, a bathroom and a kitchen. You should bring whatever food you'll need. A wood stove provides heat, and firewood is stacked on the deck. Part of the deal is that the Hammetts give you the use of a car while you're a guest; the tank is full when you arrive, and you fill it when you leave. The car is essential, since much of what you'll do at Stehekin is centered around the North Cascades Lodge, which is a ways down the road. There you can rent horses, boats, bicycles, go on guided nature walks or on a float trip. In the winter, cross-country skiing and snowshoeing are excellent. For ideas on places to eat in the Stehekin area, see the listing under North Cascades Lodge below.

Comments

"At the landing, the Park Service has a visitor center with exhibits, lectures, and guided walks. They also run a shuttle bus that provides service to many trail heads for one-day hikes. We felt lucky to have the Hammetts' car, so we didn't have to stick to the shuttle schedule which might be hard with tired children."

"Be sure to pack plenty of food. The general store isn't very well stocked, and mostly has things like candy and pop for day-boat passengers."

North Cascades Lodge

Stehekin, WA 98852
509-682-4711
Moderate to Expensive—$45-$80 for lodging plus cost of boat ($17
round trip for adults, $8.50 for kids); or plane ($21 each passenger
each way) from Chelan
MC, V

Directions: From Chelan, take "Lady of the Lake" boat or fly by
charter to Stehekin on Chelan Airways, Inc.

At A Glance: Cribs; Kitchens; TV (in lounge); Restaurant; Hot tub;
Horseback riding; Bicycle rentals; Hiking trails; Skiing (cross-country);
Fishing rentals; Boat rentals; River rafting; Moped rentals

Stehekin is really out in the boonies: only a handful of families live
here year-round, and the children go to the only one-room schoolhouse left in the state of Washington. Everything is brought in by
barge, and there are no phones. Needless to say, it makes a quiet
and relaxing vacation spot, but getting there is a challenge. The trip
up Lake Chelan on "Lady of the Lake" takes four hours. A quicker
but more expensive route is to fly in. In the winter, the lodge is open
for cross-country skiing, which is excellent (average snowfall
November-March is four feet), but the boat only goes up the lake two
or three times a week, so plan your trip carefully.

There are lodge rooms and cabins; some units have housekeeping
facilities and some have fireplaces. All are comfortable and simply appointed. Maid service is prompt and the staff is friendly and helpful.

In the summer, good weather is almost guaranteed. The water is
very cold, but riding, hiking and boating activities are endless. The
National Park Service offers many free programs, including slide
shows, bus service to scenic points, and nature walks. Some of the
latter are specifically designed with children in mind—they're short,
and include stops at the one-room schoolhouse and apple juice at the
Ranger's house. A local community center offers square dancing and
movies.

If you rent a housekeeping unit, be sure to bring your food with
you, as supplies at Stehekin are expensive. The grocery store does
sell good sandwiches for lunch. The restaurant at the lodge is fine for
breakfast, has a rather limited menu for dinner, and is moderately expensive. A fun trip for a meal is to Stehekin Valley Ranch, owned by
the Courtney family. The ranch will provide van service out and back
from the lodge, or you can take a taxi. Dinner is served buffet style
with a different main dish every night, with hamburgers and steaks as

alternates. Everything is cooked on a wood stove, including wonderful pie, and all guests eat together at big log tables in a pole frame kitchen and dining room, roofed, but with open air walls and a view of the corrals and alfalfa fields. Coffee is available on a campfire. There are no high chairs, but kids are very welcome.

A mile and a half up the road from Stehekin Landing is The Honey Bear Bakery, a backwoods operation in a shack-like building that looks more like someone's storage shed than a business. The cinnamon rolls, cookies and breads are delicious.

Comments

"Stehekin has a wonderful calm atmosphere. The Lodge acts as a comfortable, friendly base from which we were able to pursue various activities. The Lodge isn't the focal point of the trip but rather a starting point for some super wilderness experiences."

Kelly's Resort

Rt. 1, Box 119, Chelan, WA 98816
509-687-3220
Moderate—$46-$70; weekly rates available
MC, V

Directions: Located north of the State Park in the South Shore Recreation Area on Twenty-Five Mile Creek Rd., 13 miles from Chelan.

At A Glance: Cribs and playpen (need to reserve); Kitchens; Fishing rentals; Boat rentals; Playground; Pets OK; Babysitting (by pre-arrangement)

Kelly's is run by a young couple with two children, and it's a very family-oriented place. It's open only in the summer, and is more rustic and less crowded than the better-known and expensive resorts in the town of Chelan. Cabins have wood stoves, are very comfortable, and are grouped together in the woods on a hill. Kitchens are fully equipped and bathrooms have showers. The lodge has an old bowling machine, a video game, a ping pong table, a fireplace, and a general store. Outdoor activities include swimming (the water is very cold in early summer), and boating in rowboats or canoes. The beach is small but safe, and you can build a bonfire at night.

Should you want to supplement your own cooking, there are a number of options in downtown Chelan, 14 miles distant. Campbell's Lodge has a children's menu, high chairs and boosters, good food and nice service. There are two good pizza joints: Company Creek Pizza, across from the city park, and Yesterday's Pizza, which is reported to have the best pizza in town.

Comments

"The atmosphere is relaxed, take-care-of-yourself. We went after Labor Day, and even in the rain it was a very peaceful getaway."

"Cabins on the hillside face the lake and are above the main south road. In summer the road is fairly busy but it has well marked crosswalks."

Wapato Point

P.O. Box 426, Manson, WA 98831
1-800-572-9531 or 509-687-9511
Expensive—$110 and up summer; $45-$65 off season
MC, V

Directions: From Chelan, take the north shore road, Rt 150, 9 miles.

At A Glance: Kitchens; TV; Restaurant; Indoor pool; Hot tub; Tennis courts; Bicycle rentals; Fishing rentals; Boat rentals; Playground; Babysitting (list available)

This is a fairly elaborate development of resort condominiums that differ in floor plans, although most have two floors. Units have kitchens with dishwashers and each is equipped with a Weber grill. Kids can catch fish in the fishing pond, ride bikes, or play in the two good playgrounds. The resort has two miles of private beachfront; it's located on a point of land that juts into Lake Chelan. The indoor swimming is an excellent set-up for families, with a large pool and a small wading pool and hot tub. There's plenty to keep a family occupied at Wapato, but if you need supplemental activities, horseback riding, golf and cross-country skiing aren't far away.

For restaurant suggestions in Chelan, see the other listings in this section.

Comments

"I think late spring or early autumn would be preferable to hot summer (if your children aren't grade school age), because of availability of units and lower prices."

"The one-bedroom units had a slippery and, in at least one case, spiral staircase between living area and bedroom: not great for small kids."

Methow Valley

Before the North Cascades Highway was built recently through rugged mountain country, the Methow Valley was a dead end destination reached only from a southern approach. As such it was an isolated paradise known mainly to miners, ranchers and sportsmen. Today the miners are gone, but ranches, old orchards and horses are still there. Newcomers are attracted by mountains, crystal-clear rivers, great outdoor sports of all kinds and a unique mixture of pioneer nostalgia and modern comforts.

The valley has a four-season climate averaging 300 days of sunshine a year and about 16 inches of rain. Mean average summer temperature is 78° and winter 19°. National forest and state range almost completely surround the valley. Visitors have a wide choice of activities for all ages: swimming, fishing, hiking, boating, river tubing and rafting, hay rides, horseback riding, cycling, tennis, golfing and other summer fun and great cross-country skiing, snowshoeing, 100 miles of snowmobiling trails, ice fishing and sledding in the winter. A major destination ski resort is in development at Early Winters at the head of the valley to take advantage of powder snow conditions linked with exceptionally late spring thawing.

Although there are several towns in the valley, Winthrop is the acknowledged hub. With wooden sidewalks and western turn-of-the-century buildings the town's main street is attractive and lively. Kids love it. The town was started in 1891 by Guy Waring, a Harvard graduate, who named it for a colonial governor of Massachusetts and then financed his trading company with money from Boston friends. A Harvard classmate, Owen Wister, visited Winthrop on his honeymoon, traveling by buggy from the railhead at Coulee City. While in Winthrop he wrote the first chapters of his famous western novel, *The Virginian*. (Do you remember Gary Cooper in the leading role drawling to the villain, "When you call me that, smile"?) Waring's log cabin home is now a friendly little museum full of touchable things from early days. Waring ran his trading company for 49 years, until 1952.

HOW TO GET THERE

There are two main routes: State Highway 20, commonly called the North Cascades Highway, and U.S. 2. NOTE: The North Cascades Highway is not open year-round. Winter weather closes it from about mid-November until spring, usually late March. To reach the valley for a winter outing use U.S. 2.

How to get on Highway 20: The North Cascades Highway begins at the junction of I-5 and Highway 20 near Burlington, about 50 miles north of Seattle. Follow Highway 20 to Mazama and Winthrop. From Seattle, 192 miles; four hours driving time.

How to get on U.S. 2: Take I-5 27 miles north from Seattle to Exit 194 near Everett. A new access route to U.S. 2 is Exit 182 about 12 miles north of Seattle on I-5. This leads to Highway 405 connecting with Highway 522 to Monroe where it joins U.S. 2. Bellevue area residents can use Highway 405 north to make the same connection with Highway 522 near Bothell. Turn north on U.S. 97 near Wenatchee. Follow the Columbia River north to the junction with Highway 153 at Pateros. Turn north on Highway 153 along the Methow River to Twisp, where the highway merges with Highway 20. From Seattle, 244 miles and five hours driving time.

Alternate route to Highway 2 via Snoqualmie Pass: From Seattle take I-90 about 100 miles to Exit 85 just east of Cle Elum for Highway 970 merging into U.S. 97. This goes through Blewett Pass in the Wenatchee Mountains to connect with U.S. 2. From Seattle, 255 miles; 5½ hours driving time.

From Portland: Take I-84 east along the Columbia River to U.S. 97 at Biggs. Cross the Columbia, follow U.S. 97 north through Goldendale, Yakima and Ellensburg through Blewett Pass to U.S. 2 and Wenatchee. Follow U.S. 97 north from Wenatchee along the Columbia River to Highway 153 at Pateros. Follow Highway 153 and Highway 20 to Winthrop. From Portland, 400 miles and 7-8 hours driving time.

WHAT TO SEE ON THE WAY

The routes to and from the Methow form the Cascade Loop. Except for winter trips when the North Cascades Highway is closed, the loop affords an opportunity to see a wide variety of spectacular scenery and interesting roadside attractions.

Beginning at the Seattle end of the loop, cross the Cascade Mountains on I-90 at Snoqualmie Pass (el. 3010 ft.) or on U.S. 2 at Stevens Pass (el. 4061 ft.). Both pass summits have skiing facilities, food service, rest rooms, and good trail hiking.

On Stevens Pass U.S. 2 goes through small towns along the Skykomish River dating from the gold mining era. They are now timber towns. On the east side of the Cascades the Bavarian-style town

of Leavenworth marks the western edge of the world-famous
Wenatchee Valley apple orchards. Leavenworth has quaint shops and
European-style festivals. A short way down the valley is Cashmere, a
spic-and-span early American town. Here is the Aplet and Cotlet Candy Kitchen where a fruit and nut confection has been made for 60
years. Visitors are welcome and the kids like the samples. The
Wenatchee River flows down this valley and like several other rivers
on this loop trip offers rafting, boating and fishing. There are many
roadside fruit stands open in season.

After you leave U.S. 2 and turn north on U.S. 97 there are two
special attractions. The Ohme Gardens, open from April through October, were developed on a high rocky bluff overlooking the Columbia
River and the Wenatchee Valley. It took 50 years by a dedicated family to build this alpine-style garden, rated as one of the outstanding
gardens in the country. Close by on U.S. 97 is Rocky Reach Dam
where you can look a salmon in the eye. Besides an attractive picnic
area there is much to see in the main building. The fish ladder viewing room is where you can observe at close range the salmon swimming upstream to return to their spawning grounds. There are also
exhibits on geology and the story of electricity.

As you proceed north you will find for sale many apple varieties un-
heard of in city stores. The growers say these apples are tastier and
you will probably agree.

If your route is the North Cascades Highway, you will pass through
the lush Skagit Valley along the rushing Skagit River, the source of
hydroelectric power for Seattle. Two towns have unusual names.
Sedro Woolley is a combination of the Spanish word for cedar and the
name of the owner of one of the pioneer lumber mills. Farther on is
Concrete, named for its limestone deposits and cement plants. A
1500-acre bird sanctuary on the Skagit River makes this one of the
prime places in the country to view bald eagles at their nesting
places. The river provides great rafting and fishing.

At Marblemount the highway starts to climb through the upper
Skagit River Valley to the Seattle City Light company town Newhalem, headquarters for three big dams. From the nearby company
town Diablo, City Light has official tours which include a famous
family-style chicken dinner. The tour is so popular that reservations
are necessary (206)625-3050. If you can't manage that, you will find
the little museum in Diablo of interest. Depending on the time of your
visit, you might be able to ride the 51-year-old incline railway, last of
its kind in the country, which was built to lift train-carloads of dam
construction materials 560 feet up the side of Sourdough Mountain.

On your own you can take half-mile loop hikes on woodland trails
starting from Newhalem.

From Diablo the new section of the North Cascades Highway is readily apparent. It is a broad, modern highway with spacious shoulders for emergency stops and frequent turnouts at scenic points and trail heads. There are stunning alpine views of mountain lakes, soaring peaks, and grassy meadowlands. At Rainy Pass (el. 4860 ft.) the highway crosses the Pacific Crest National Scenic Trail stretching from Canada to Mexico. At Washington Pass (el. 5447 ft.) there is a spectacular scenic viewpoint of surrounding peaks before you drop down into the Methow Valley.

Idle-a-While Motel

Box 575, Twisp, WA 98856
509-997-3222
Inexpensive—$27-$33 per night; $3 per extra person
AE, MC, V

Directions: Located on Hwy 20, ¼ mile north of Twisp.

At A Glance: Cribs; Kitchens; TV; Sauna; Hot tub; Skiing trails; Tennis court; Pets OK; Babysitting (by pre-arrangement).

Don't be put off by Idle-a-While's plain appearance; it's clean, service is excellent and it meets all basic needs. Of the 25 motel units, three are two-bedroom cottages and 13 others also have kitchens. Although located on a highway, it is not noisy and the road traffic is light.

Idle-a-While is an inexpensive alternative to better-known places such as the nearby Sun Mountain Lodge. The owner is an avid cross-country skier and he grooms several miles of trails which begin at his front door. Many of these trails are flat and thus perfect for first-time skiers. An added bonus—sledding is excellent behind the motel.

Comments
"The owner seemed especially concerned about his trail conditions for little first-timers."

North Cascades Base Camp

Star Route, Box 36, Mazama, WA 98833
509-996-2334
Inexpensive—$24-$33 adults; $17-$19 ages 7-12; $12-$14 ages 4-6; un-
der 4 free; prices include lodging and all meals
No credit cards

Directions: Hwy 20 to Mazama. At the Mazama Store, head northwest on Lost River Rd 2.2 miles. North Cascades Base Camp is on
the left.

At A Glance: Playpen (for use as crib): TV; Restaurant; Hot tub;
Ski trails; Skating rink; Play yard; Babysitting (by pre-arrangement).

Sue and Dick Roberts have built a wonderful inn in a beautiful setting with a set-up that is great for families with children. They rent
out a room with a double bed and four- and six-person rooms with
bunk beds, all with shared bath. It's hard to get a reservation here in
the winter—it's been discovered by families who love the cross-
country skiing in the Methow Valley—but in summer it's easier.

The Robertses have two kids of their own, so the place is geared
to children. A huge sandbox converts in winter to a skating rink, and
they have plenty of skates for you to borrow. There are also swings
and a playhouse, and a swimming hole and trout pond are under development a short walk away. The Base Camp land borders the river,
so it's easy to reach, but not so close as to be dangerous. Indoors,
there are a playroom with plenty of toys, a library, and lots of games
and magazines.

All meals are included with a stay at the Base Camp, and they are
healthy and tasty. Breakfast and dinner are served, and lunch fixings
are put out for you to make your own. The Robertses recommend
the Mountain Song Cafe in Marblemount, about 100 miles west on
Route 20, as a good place to stop on your way to or from their inn in
the summer. The homemade pies and ice cream are delicious and kids
are welcome.

Comments

"A perfect place for a family vacation to the almost wilderness; you
get a bed, meals and all conveniences for a reasonable price. Kids are
welcomed and enjoyed. We had no desire to even get in our car for
the four days we were there."

"The Robertses are very familiar with the area and can tell about
hikes and expeditions with their children."

"There is no smoking in the inn. We were pleased."

Sun Mountain Lodge

P.O. Box 1000, Winthrop, WA 98862
1-800-572-0493; 509-996-2211
Expensive—$60-$100 per night; $5 per extra person over 6 years old
AE, CB, DC, MC, V

Directions: From Hwy 20, just east of Winthrop, follow signs 12 miles to the lodge.

At A Glance: Cribs; Game room; TV (in lodge); Restaurant; Outdoor pool; Hot tub; Horseback riding; Tennis courts; Hiking trails; Lawn games; Skiing trails; Boat rentals; Fishing rentals; Playground; Pets OK; Organized activities for kids; Babysitting (by pre-arrangement).

By the time you complete the drive to the top of Sun Mountain, you'll be convinced you're in God's country. This resort is situated to give an incredible view of high snow-capped mountain peaks as well as the entire expanse of the Methow Valley. Yearly precipitation at Sun Mountain is only about 15 inches a year, and most of that is snow (averages 3-4 feet during the winter), so summers are dry and good weather is the norm.

Sun Mountain consists of 40 units—two are suites with fireplaces and mini-refrigerators. The rooms, which have a queen-size bed and two twins, are in two buildings—one group has a view down to Patterson Lake, the other a better one to the mountains. The swimming pool, located next to the lodge, has marine fossils in its rock walls, preserved when hot lava spilled from the sea bottom when the Methow Valley was under the ocean.

Activities vary according to the season, and organized programs for kids are available upon request, with a minimum of 24 hours notice. In summer, there are hiking trails of ½ to 2½ miles; some of these are marked with placards that give interesting nature information. Hayrides are also offered, followed by a picnic or barbecue. In the winter, there are 50 miles of marked cross-country ski trails; 30 of these are groomed.

One of the few drawbacks to Sun Mountain Lodge is the restaurant situation. Although the dining room, cantilevered over the Methow Valley, gives a beautiful setting for a meal, the food is expensive and mediocre. The only alternative is the 12-mile trip into Winthrop.

Comments

"The setting is spectacular and activities endless. If I could afford to, I'd spend all summer there."

The Virginian

Winthrop, WA 98862
509-996-2535
Inexpensive—$35-$55; $5-$7 per extra person
AE, MC, V

Directions: Located on Hwy 20, just east of Winthrop.

At A Glance: Kitchens; TV; Restaurant; Outdoor pool (seasonal);
Ski trails

The Virginian offers a variety of accommodations: cabins with small
kitchens, some eight-plexes with very large rooms, and a row of
motel units with smaller rooms. Rollaways are available at $5 per
night. The place is built out of logs, which lends it a rustic western
feeling. However, the rooms are new and modern and have good
bathrooms. (Cabins have only showers.) Two grocery stores are located right next door—a good place for kids to get "treats."

The informal and friendly setting at the Virginian makes it an obvi-
ous choice for a family. Cross-country ski trails begin behind the hotel
and follow the Methow River; others begin across the street. In summer, the small outdoor pool gives relief from the dry heat.

The restaurant at the Virginian is casual and the food is gourmet.
There is a children's menu for kids under 12 with a choice of chicken,
spaghetti or fish served with soup or salad. Prices are reasonable.

Comments
"Our family goes to the Winthrop/Twisp area at least twice a year,
and the Virginian is always the children's favorite place to stay."

North Cascades

The North Cascade Mountain range is sometimes called the American Alps. The rugged snow-capped mountains, glaciers, lakes and waterfalls provide alpine vistas for sightseers and challenging country for hikers. The area has become known to more people since the opening of the North Cascades Highway. However, winter snows close Highway 20 from fall to spring from a point about six miles east of Diablo Lake.

The Diablo Lake area is in the Seattle City Light hydroelectric development comprising three dams on the Skagit River. Tours operated by City Light include a boat trip across Diablo Lake, a walk through the Ross Dam powerhouse, and a fabulous family-style chicken dinner. For tour reservations call Seattle City Light, (206)625-3050.

Depending on the season the Diablo area offers a wide range of outdoor activities. Because it is only 2½ hours driving time from Seattle, it is a hub point from which to see several beautiful parts of the North Cascades on a short visit. Or it can be a convenient stop on the way across the North Cascades Highway to the Methow Valley.

HOW TO GET THERE
Take I-5 north about 50 miles to Exit 232 to Highway 20, just north of Mt. Vernon. Follow Highway 20 to the Newhalem-Diablo area.

WHAT TO SEE ON THE WAY
The highway through the fertile Skagit Valley and along the rushing Skagit River has many attractive stopping places. A 1500-acre bird sanctuary on the river makes this a prime region for viewing bald eagles. The river is noted for fishing and for rafting. At Newhalem, City Light's company town, there are woodland hikes and nature trails. A few miles farther is Diablo which has an interesting little pioneer museum. This is where the tours start.

Diablo Lake Resort

Diablo, Rockport, WA 98283
Call your operator and ask for the Everett, WA, operator to ring
Newhalem 5578.
Inexpensive—$45 for 2 people; $10 for each additional person; ages 15
and under $5
AE, MC, V

Directions: I-5 to Mt. Vernon Exit 232, Cook Rd. East on Hwy 20
for 68 miles. The resort is off Hwy 20 between Diablo Dam (drive
across the dam itself to reach the resort) and Ross Dam.

At A Glance: Kitchens; Restaurant; Fishing rentals; Boat rentals;
Hiking trails; Pets OK ($5)

If you're hooked on North Cascades scenery, this is a good place to
spend a night or two to absorb some of it close up. To get to the
resort, you get to drive across the top of huge Diablo Dam, which is
fun in itself. The place is right on the lake formed by the top of the
dam, and tall mountains come right down to the water.

The resort has 20 one-, two- or three-bedroom cabins, fully
equipped for housekeeping. The larger cabins can easily accommodate
two families, and, while exteriors look a little worn, interiors are
scrupulously clean.

Fishing is terrific year round, boats can be rented at the resort's
marina. A good short excursion is to Monkey Island, in the middle of
Diablo Lake, where you can pull your boat on shore and explore. A
well-maintained trail from the resort to Ross Dam is a good family
hike of 3½ miles.

If you plan to cook in your cabin, bring your food, as the small
grocery has a limited selection and high prices. Coffee and rolls are
available in the office. The resort's restaurant, The Hidden Inn, has a
lovely setting and serves basic food—slowly.

Comments

"To get out of the car and look over the edge of Diablo Dam is an
unforgettable experience."

"We found the carcass of a deer on Monkey Island and the children
were fascinated. It's the perfect size island for exploration and
picnicking—makes you feel like Huckleberry Finn."

IDAHO

North Idaho

It is a long drive from Seattle to the lakes and forests of the Idaho panhandle (six to eight hours depending on stops), but that does not diminish the enthusiasm families have for this corner of the Pacific Northwest. It is definitely summer country at its best from the Fourth of July to Labor Day. The days are hot and sunny. If you can afford to fly to Spokane and rent a car for the rest of the trip the travel time shrinks to long weekend proportions. Otherwise it has to be considered vacation area for a stay of a week or longer.

Priest Lake is a large, deep, clear, beautiful body of water. Great for boating, canoeing and swimming, although it is somewhat cool until late in the summer. Because of its size boating safety precautions must be observed in case a summer squall suddenly occurs.

One of the distinctive treats of this location is the huckleberry picking in August. The berries are the best. This is a rare treat because these berries are scarce in markets and it is fun for all the family to pick them, eat them heartily and take large quantities home. A local ranger station will tell you where the picking is good.

HOW TO GET THERE

The fastest route from Seattle to Spokane is I-90. However, there are opportunities to switch over to U.S. 2 in order to see some interesting places. For example, you can leave I-90 at George and go north on Highway 283 to Ephrata and Soap Lake. From Soap Lake you can take Highway 28 to Davenport and Spokane, or turn north on Highway 17 to see Sun Lakes State Park and, farther north, the Grand Coulee Dam. From these points you can swing back to U.S. 2 to Spokane.

From Spokane take Highway 2 to Newport and Priest River, turning north on Highway 57 at Priest River to Nordman and Priest Lake.

WHAT TO SEE ON THE WAY

There are all sorts of interesting places to visit on a trip across the state. On I-90 the Gingko Petrified Forest State Park and museum at

Vantage, on a bluff overlooking the Columbia River, is an education in the unusual geology of the area. Soap Lake is a once renowned spa where people tried the medicinal effects of the hot mineral baths. The lake itself has a soapy feel and produces "soapsuds" along the shore. It offers an enjoyable swim break on a long hot drive across the state. North from Soap Lake is Sun Lakes State Park with good swimming and picnic areas. From here it is an easy detour to Grand Coulee Dam, a spectacular monument to hydroelectric power well worth seeing. Spokane's Riverfront Park, former site of Expo '74, is worth visiting if only to see and ride a wonderful old carousel with carved wood figures.

Elkins Resort

Box 40, Route 1, Nordman, ID 83848
208-443-2432
Moderate—$525 per week for a 2-bedroom cabin
MC, V

Directions: From Spokane take U.S. 2 north to Newport and Priest River. At Priest River turn north on Rt 57 to Nordman (37 miles). At Nordman, turn right and go about 2 miles.

At A Glance: Cribs; Kitchens; Restaurant; Hiking trails; Boat rentals; Surfsailer rentals; Cross-country ski rentals; Snowmobile trails

When you stay at Elkins Resort, you live in rustic log cabins on a bluff overlooking Priest Lake. Cabins have kitchens and baths and are situated for privacy. It's an old-fashioned type of resort (it's been around 30 years or more) that caters mainly to families. The chances are good that children will find others to pal around with.

The beach at the resort is nice and sandy, with a long drop-off. Access to the beach is via trails from the bluff (about 100 ft.). Swimming, canoeing, huckleberry picking and hiking are warm-weather activities at Priest Lake. Indoors there is a game room. A small store has groceries and gift items. Elkins is in the mountains, and weather can be variable, with occasional exciting thundershowers and rainbows.

There is a restaurant in the lodge if you don't want to cook all your meals in the cabin kitchen. Prices are moderate, food is good, and children are tolerated well. For food shopping plan to stop at the Safeway in Newport.

Comments
"We generally 'hit the beach' on nice days and canoe, or we hike if the weather is cloudy. This resort is probably best for families with children ages 5-12. Babies and toddlers would need to be watched carefully at the lake—no lifeguard—and might not enjoy hiking."

Hill's Resort

Box 162A, Route 5, Priest Lake, ID 83856
208-443-2551
Moderate—Summer: $325-$650 per week (sleeps 4-10 people);
September-June: nightly rates $33-$93 (2-10 people)
MC, V

Directions: From Spokane go north on U.S. 2 through Newport to Priest River. Turn north on Hwy 57 to Priest Lake.

At A Glance: Cribs; Kitchens; Restaurant; Tennis courts; Hiking trails; Ski trails; Fishing rentals; Boat rentals; Babysitting (by pre-arrangement); Pets OK

There are about 50 units of various sizes and with various accoutrements at Hill's, but the best deal for small families is the cheaper ($325 per week) housekeeping cabins. They don't have fireplaces or views, but you don't really need these, as all cabins let you see a little of the lake and are close to the water. The beach has numerous firepits.

Hill's is a family-oriented and family-run resort. Most guests have been coming back for years, and kids outnumber adults. There are usually lots of toddlers and babies. Guests are very friendly with each other.

Unless you come for snowmobiling and cross-country skiing in the winter, July and August are good months to visit this resort. Days are long and Priest Lake has had a chance to warm up a little. It's a good lake for water sports and the beach is huge, sandy and picturesque. On Monday nights, there are movies on the beach, on Thursdays a family barbecue.

There is a dining room at Hill's which is really nice; if you take children, go early. They do have booster seats and high chairs. There is no children's menu, but they have hamburgers and chicken and are willing to split an order. The huckleberry pie is terrific. Another option is to go 20 miles north to Elkins Resort, where the eating situation is similar but cozier, and where there's a children's menu. There are no large grocery stores nearby—the best bets for shopping are large markets in Priest River or Newport, at a distance of 60 miles.

Comments

"Hill's is not near other parks, lakes or places to visit if you get restless and want to sightsee."

"A relaxed and relaxing place without a lot of the hustle and bustle of busier places. A good place to play, sleep, sun, read on the beach, have cookouts, visit with other parents and grandparents, spend a quiet post-bedtime hour in the lounge, and enjoy the quiet blue water of Priest Lake. We're going back!"

OREGON

Oregon Coast

The Oregon coast beaches are scenic, sandy and lots of fun. The driving time to some is about the same for Seattle area residents as the Washington coast beaches.

Washington and Oregon coasts are similar in many ways— mountains, lakes, rivers and broad sandy ocean beaches that are easily accessible. Oregon's coast is very open, and there are sizable towns offering "rain insurance" attractions— entertaining things to do regardless of the weather.

Best known of the scores of developed areas are Seaside and Cannon Beach on the north end, easily reached from the metropolitan Seattle and Portland areas. Other beaches to the south are also readily accessible with just a little more easy driving through beautiful countryside. Highway 101 hugs the coast the entire length of the state.

This region is not for wilderness hiking or roughing it. Oregon beaches are easy fun and enjoyment. Every area has special attractions such as Haystack Rock, the third largest monolith in the world, south of Cannon Beach. This and many other areas have exceptional tide pools at low tide. Everywhere are quirky little shops that are heavenly for kids with a couple of dollars to spend. The civilized conditions also mean numerous well-equipped state parks that dot the area, municipal swimming pools, golf courses, tennis courts and playgrounds.

The coast reeks of western history from the days of sailing ships and overland explorations. These are well-documented by monuments and museums. Specific information is abundant in handouts and guide books available everywhere.

HOW TO GET THERE

From the Seattle area take I-5 south. The fastest route to the Seaside and Cannon Beach areas leaves I-5 at Longview-Kelso, takes Highway 433 across the Columbia River bridge at Longview, and

connects with Highway 30 to Astoria, Oregon, where U.S. 101 is
picked up. Travel time from Seattle is about 4½ to 5 hours.

An alternate route is I-5 to Portland, then Highway 26 to Cannon
Beach or alternate routes to the central coast. There are several
clearly designated routes from I-5 west to the coast.

WHAT TO SEE ON THE WAY

The state capital buildings in Olympia, 60 miles south of Seattle on
I-5, are worth a look. The capitol, copied from the national capitol in
Washington, D.C., contains the legislative chambers and also the
offices of the governor, lieutenant governor, secretary of state and
state treasurer. All are open to visitors during business hours. On the
south side of the capitol is the state library with an interesting mural
by Kenneth Callahan and a collection of works by state authors. On
the north side of the capitol is the state supreme court building.

South of Chehalis signs of the Mount St. Helens eruptions can be
seen where the highway crosses the Toutle River. Huge mounds of
mud and debris dredged from the river line the bank of the Columbia
River. There are several turnoffs to reach Mount St. Helens National
Volcanic Monument points of interest, including observation outlooks
to see what's left of the mountain peak.

If your route is through Longview you will pass through St. Helens,
Oregon, en route to Astoria. Boise Cascade Corporation offers tours
of its paper mill here. Call Diane Dillard at (503)397-2900 in advance
to get details.

If you stay on I-5 to Portland you may visit the Boise Cascade
paper mill at Vancouver, Washington. Call Carole Dunn at
(206)693-2567 in advance.

If your route is through Astoria, the Columbia River Maritime
Museum there is rated the top museum of its kind in the Pacific
Northwest.

Depending on your route and destination there are some other good
places to watch for along the coast: Ecola State Park near Cannon
Beach, a cheese factory in Tillamook, Cape Meares Loop Trip, Sea
Lion Caves, Heceta Head Lighthouse and Seal Rock State Park.

Driftwood Shores

88416 First Ave., Florence, OR 97439
503-997-8263
Moderate—$40-$55; $5 per extra person
AE, DC, MC, V

Directions: From Portland, take any highway west to Oregon coast. Then take U.S. 101 south to Florence. Hotel is located 4 miles north of town, west of U.S. 101 along Heceta Beach Rd.

At A Glance: Cribs; Kitchens; TV; Restaurant; Indoor pool; Sauna; Hot tub

This oceanfront resort motel has 136 units, of which 25 are three-bedroom units and 21 are two-bedroom units. Most have kitchens, lots have fireplaces (and firewood), and some suites come with two bathrooms. It's comfortable and clean, but not fancy. Decks overlook the beach, which is lovely and long. In rainy weather, when the beach is cold, it's nice to be able to fall back on the indoor swimming facilities. There's a laundromat on the premises to dry wet bathing suits.

The restaurant at Driftwood Shores has moderate prices and unremarkable food. They've got high chairs and the service is good. In the town of Florence, the Windward Inn has great food, particularly seafood and homemade desserts. There is a gift shop in the restaurant that children will love. On your way to or from the Oregon coast, try stopping at Ducky Waddles, off I-5 in Portland. It's a real old-fashioned hamburger joint, 50's vintage, with rounded booths and malt shop atmosphere. They have a children's menu, boosters and high chairs, and they love kids.

Comments
"This was a relaxing place with just enough diversion to keep everyone from getting tired of the beach. We did spend hours and hours on the long stretches of sandy, driftwood-strewn beach and loved it."

"The staff was friendly and accommodating."

Edgewater Cottages

8400 Hwy 101, Waldport, OR 97394
503-563-2240
Inexpensive—$22-$44
No credit cards

Directions: I-5 through Portland. At Albany take Hwy 20 west. At Newport go south on U.S. 101 to Waldport.

At A Glance: Cribs; Kitchens; TV; Pets OK ($2); Babysitting (by pre-arrangement)

This is a lodging that books up early, especially in the summer and all holidays. Comprised of a four-plex, a duplex and several individual cabins, Edgewater is situated on a wonderful expanse of very safe beach. Though it's close to the highway, the focus is definitely towards the beach. Cabins are comfortable, with fireplaces and decent beds, fully stocked kitchens and cable TV. Cabin size and prices vary according to the number of people: for one of the larger cabins that will hold several people, the cost is about $67 to $82 per night. There's an area of lawn for frisbee or soccer, and beach access via stairs. An old tree stump on the beach is perfect for playing ship or fort.

Lots of vendors in the harbor at Newport, 15 miles north, sell fresh, live crab—a delicious treat that you can cook in your Edgewater kitchen.

Comments

"The managers were very accommodating, but they couldn't do anything about a few minor inconveniences: the bathroom never dried out between showers, the hide-a-bed was horrible, they were short on pillows, and the firewood was wet."

"Edgewater Cottages is a great spot and satisfied all of us, ages 8 months to 10 years and up."

The Sea Sprite

Tolovana Park, OR 97145
503-436-2266
Moderate—$40-$86 for 2-8 people; winter: $30-$80; off-season specials
MC, V

Directions: I-5 to Portland, then west on Hwy 26, west on Hwy 6, north on U.S. 101. Or, I-5 to Kelso, cross the Columbia River at Longview to Hwy 30 to Astoria, then go south on U.S. 101.

At A Glance: Cribs; Kitchens; TV

The Sea Sprite is located in the quiet part of Cannon Beach, a ten-minute walk south of Haystack Rock, where tidepool life abounds at low tide. Decor is comfortable and homey, complete with rocking chairs and fireplaces. All units are supplied with firewood, and kitchens are fully equipped. Of the six available units, two are for two people, two will accommodate up to five people, one up to six, and the last, a separate two-bedroom cottage, will hold up to eight people. There are picnic tables and flower gardens on the grounds. Because of the small size of the Sea Sprite, it's a good idea to make reservations in plenty of time, especially for the summer.

Two good eating stops on the way to the Sea Sprite are The Ship Inn in Astoria, which is on the railroad tracks and has a view of the Columbia, and Christopher's in Kelso, which has a choice of fancy dining room or lunch counter. Once at the Sea Sprite, The Brass Lantern is a family-style place with Middle Eastern specialties, high chairs and a good Sunday brunch. It's located ten blocks south of downtown Cannon Beach on Hemlock. (For other suggestions see listing under Surfsand.) If you're out exploring the coast to the south, try Roseanna's Cafe, on Highway 131 in Oceanside, 40 miles south of the Sea Sprite. It's right near a nice protected beach and has good burgers, quiche and seafood soups.

Comments
"Things to do: beach, beach, beach."

Surfsand Best Western

1080 Ecola Court/P.O. Box 219, Cannon Beach, OR 97110
503-436-2274
Moderate to Expensive—$39-$119
AE, DC, MC, V

Directions: I-5 south to Kelso-Longview, crossing Columbia River on
Rt 433. Take U.S. 30 to Astoria, where you get on U.S. 101 south to
Cannon Beach. Located one block west of Beach Loop Rd., at the
foot of Gower St.

At A Glance: Cribs; Kitchens; TV; Indoor pool; Hot tub

This two-story, 40-unit motel is not particularly attractive, but it's
right on the ocean, has good service and nice people running it. One-
and two-bedroom housekeeping units with kitchens and fireplaces run
$99-$109 a day. Wood is left at your door, as is the morning paper.
It's hard to get reservations, particularly in the summer.

Access to the beach is excellent—you can see your children digging
in the sand while you have a cup of coffee on your balcony. The
beach is wide and good for kite flying and playing in the tidepools at
Haystack Rock, located just to the south of Surfsand. The indoor
swimming pool is never very crowded and has a slide into it and stairs
for young children to play on. On Saturday nights in the summer
there are wiener roasts around a beach fire.

If you do get a housekeeping unit, bring your food with you; Cannon Beach has limited grocery shopping facilities. The Wanderer is
the restaurant owned by Surfsand, located across the street. There is
a children's menu, and high chairs and boosters are available. Prices
are moderate to expensive and service is a bit slow. If you want to go
into Cannon Beach proper, you can walk down along the beach and
then cut into town to The Lemon Tree. This is a casual restaurant
with good basic food (particularly breakfast) and high kid tolerance.
The Cannon Beach Bakery has Haystack Bread and sweet rolls, and
children can watch the bakers working through the window early in
the day. For more suggestions, see the listing under Sea Sprite.

Comments

"It's fun for little kids to feed the seagulls leftovers on the
balcony."

"Surfsand is wonderful anytime—the ocean is so close. We love this
place."

New Surfview Resort

1400 S. Hemlock/P.O. Box 547, Cannon Beach, OR 97110
1-800-547-6423; in Oregon 1-800-453-7132
Expensive—$62-$215 (for 2-8 people)
AE, MC, V

Directions: From Portland, west on U.S. 26 to U.S. 101, then south 4 miles. Or, I-5 south to Longview, west on Hwy 433 across the Columbia River to Hwy 30 to Astoria, then south on U.S. 101. Located ½ mile south off Beach Loop Rd., at Hemlock.

At A Glance: Cribs; Kitchens; TV; Restaurant; Indoor pool; Sauna; Hot tub

This is a new complex, built on top of the dunes just opposite Haystack Rock. It's all clean, modern and attractive. Units come in all different sizes, with various sleeping configurations. Typical accommodations for four would be a living room with fireplace, lanai, and pull-down Sico bed, kitchen, bathroom, and separate bedroom with twins or queen for about $100.

Beach access is via a wooden staircase that takes you down the bluff. The beach is lovely and wide, and the tidepools at Haystack Rock, replete with starfish and sea anemones, are just in front of the motel. Seagulls frequent the balconies and you can sit in your living room at night with a fire going and hear the ocean outside your window. Firewood is provided outside each room, and the morning paper is delivered each day.

On rainy days or in the winter when the beach is less hospitable, families can take advantage of the indoor swimming facilities. The pool has a sliding board and stairs, and there is a separate wading pool for little people. Adults can use the hot tub, sauna and exercise room.

For eating suggestions in Cannon Beach, see the listings under Surfsand and Sea Sprite above.

Comments

"The pool had too much chlorine. The children's eyes stung."

"The wall bed in the living room is such a good idea. We housed the kids in the bedroom, and then were able to enjoy the ocean and fireplace from the living room after they'd gone to bed. It was also great having two TVs."

Central Oregon

Oregon has two distinctly different climates caused by the Cascade Mountain Range. The lush, wet coastal area on the west side of the Cascades contrasts with dry and sunny high country on the east side. In Central Oregon there is a wide range of year-round recreational activities linked to a varied geography: skiing in winter; swimming, hiking, rock-hounding in summer. It is open country readily accessible by car. The distances from the metropolitan area of Portland are not great, and Seattle is only 180 miles away, 3½ hours driving time on I-5 South.

A trip to central Oregon offers opportunities to get better acquainted with the majestic Columbia River. On the way to central Oregon resorts, it is easy to make a loop around Mount Hood in order to drive the spectacular Columbia River Gorge where the river slices through the Cascades. High waterfalls tumble along the highway. River vistas are similar to the Rhine. Orchards flourish where the land slopes up from the river.

The shapely cone of 11,235-foot Mount Hood is the main attraction and there are other peaks over 10,000 feet on the central plateau, such as Mount Jefferson and the Three Sisters. Lofty peaks all in the same family as Washington's Baker, Rainier and Adams.

Oregon has many great rivers offering boating, rafting and fishing. The main stream in central Oregon is the Deschutes River.

Whether you choose a place on the Columbia River or Mount Hood or the semi-arid and sunny stretches along the Deschutes, you will have an enjoyable experience.

HOW TO GET THERE

There are two main approaches from the Seattle area to Mount Hood and Central Oregon. One is through Portland and the other is across Snoqualmie Pass through Ellensburg, Yakima, Goldendale and Biggs, Oregon, on the Columbia River.

The fastest route from Seattle to the Mount Hood area is I-5 south to Portland, 180 miles, 3½ hours driving time, and then an additional 55 miles on Highway 26 to the south side of Mount Hood. From Portland, Hood River is 60 miles, one hour driving.

Using the alternate route across Snoqualmie Pass, the distance to Hood River is about 370 miles, five hours driving time. From just east of Hood River take Highway 35 south to connect with Highway 26. From this junction you can go west to the Mount Hood area or south to connect with U.S. 97, the main north-south artery through Central Oregon.

There are also good highways east from I-5 to the Bend area from Salem, Albany and Eugene. The shortest route is Highway 20 east from Albany.

WHAT TO SEE ON THE WAY

The 60-mile stretch from Portland to Hood River through the Columbia River Gorge on I-84 and U.S. 30 has many interesting and scenic stopping places for short hikes, spectacular views and short tours. The two highways parallel the river, but at different elevations; U.S. 30 is the upper level, the first paved highway in the state, built around 1915 to follow the contours of the land. As such it is more scenic than the modern I-84 freeway built at river level. Some of the cliffs are 2000 feet high. This feature produces spectacular waterfalls, the highest being Multnomah, a small stream falling hundreds of feet.

Bridal Veil is a lumber town known for its monolithic rock peaks and its spectacular waterfall, one of eleven such cascades between Portland and Hood River. The old Crown Point Vista House which provides views up and down the gorge has been a noted stopping place for decades.

The town of Cascade Locks has a 200-acre riverfront park with a museum that contains Oregon's first locomotive. A sternwheeler offers two-hour narrated cruises through the gorge.

A cluster of activities carry the Bonneville name. Adjacent to the dam is the Bonneville fish hatchery which has rearing ponds and a museum featuring unusual marine life. Exit 40 off I-84 leads to the Bradford Island Visitor Center for Bonneville Dam and Lock. The Center houses five floors of displays, a two-level observation deck, a three-screen theater and an underwater viewing room to observe migrating fish moving up the fish ladder.

The alternate route through Snoqualmie Pass, Ellensburg, Yakima and Goldendale also has some unusual roadside attractions. Well worth seeing near Goldendale is the Maryhill Museum of Art built by an early day railroad tycoon on a lonely site overlooking the Columbia River. To get there take Highway 14 about three miles west of the junction with U.S. 97. Coming on this massive building on attractive grounds in the middle of nowhere is a unique experience. The museum, open from March 15 to November 15, contains a large collection of original Rodin sculptures, European and American art, early Indian artifacts, unusual chess sets and personal possessions, including a throne chair of Queen Marie of Romania who created quite a stir when when she visited the place in the 1920s.

In the same area, one mile east of the junction of U.S. 97 and Highway 14, is a replica of the 4000-year-old Stonehenge near Wiltshire, England. Our Stonehenge is now a World War II memorial.

The area just south of Bend on U.S. 97 has many unusual rock formations caused by ancient volcanic eruptions and lava flows. Seven miles south of Bend on U.S. 97 is the Oregon High Desert Museum. It is a living museum of birds, mammals and plants as well as cultural and natural history exhibits telling the story of the area. It is open daily year-round.

The Lava Butte Geological Area is ten miles south of Bend on U.S. 97. Lava Butte, 500 feet high, is a good example of the numerous volcanoes that were active about 6000 years ago. Three miles farther south on U.S. 97 and nine miles east on a forest road is the Lava Cast Forest Geological Area. Along a nature trail can be seen the molds of trees engulfed in lava.

Twelve miles south of Bend on U.S. 97 are the Lava River Caves. The Lava River Tunnel is nearly a mile long. Forest rangers are on duty in the summer.

Newberry Crater is 24 miles south of Bend on U.S. 97 and 13 miles east on Paulina Lake Road. The crater has two parts separated by cinder cones. Pauline Lake and East Lake are good for fishing.

East of Bend on U.S. 20 is Pilot Butte State Park. The 500-foot cinder cone is a great viewpoint for the Cascades.

Black Butte Ranch

P.O. Box 8000, Black Butte Ranch, OR 97759
503-595-6211
Expensive—$50-$90 for rooms and suites; $100-$140 for private homes;
$110 for two-bedroom apartment with kitchen; weekly rates; 10% less off
season
AE, MC, V

Directions: From Salem on I-5 take Hwy 22 east to Hwy 20. Go through Santiam Pass about 20 miles to Black Butte. Or, take I-84 to Hood River. Take Hwy 35 south to U.S. 26. Take U.S. 26 to Madras then U.S. 97 south to Redmond. Take Hwy 126 west and go 7 miles west from Sisters.

At A Glance: Cribs; Kitchens; TV; Restaurant; Outdoor pools (4); Saunas; Horseback riding; Tennis courts; Bicycle rentals; Canoe rentals; Golf; Lawn games; Hiking trails; Babysitting (by pre-arrangement); Organized activities for kids

The units at Black Butte are individually owned, so furnishings vary, but they're well designed and are geared to accommodate families. Several units have a third bedroom that can be included with the rental if needed or closed off, reducing the rate. All units have kitchens. There is a two-night minimum for condominiums and a four-night minimum for private homes in peak season. Note: Travel agents can't book at the ranch—you have to make your own arrangements.

The setting of this 1800-acre resort is quite spectacular. A large meadow runs through the middle of the ranch and there are snow-capped peaks on the horizon. Black Butte was a family-owned cattle ranch from the late 1800s until 1970 and is still a working cattle operation. In the summer the climate is warm and dry, and in winter you can usually count on snow for skiing at nearby Hoo Doo Bowl or Mt. Bachelor.

The range of things to do at Black Butte is impressive, for both children and adults. Guests can fly fish, with barbless hooks, and fish must be released. There are 16 tennis courts, two of which are lighted; use of them is free, but reservations are needed. Two golf courses, 16 miles of bike paths, four swimming pools (located at strategic sites to decentralize activity), riding, canoeing, hiking, even white water rafting can keep a family busy for days in the summer. There's a Recreation Barn, and there are planned activities for all ages. When was the last time you played Capture the Flag or made Noodle Jewelry? Movies are shown on Friday and Saturday nights for $1.

The dining room is excellent, but you need reservations for dinner. There are snack shops by the main pool and the golf clubhouses, which are good for lunch. The Tumalo Emporium, located 24 miles southeast of Black Butte in Tumalo, is a reasonably good restaurant. They have a children's menu and offer a buffet. They can handle large groups, seating everyone together. They have a fresh fruit cobbler that you should order as soon as you get there as it sells out early.

Comments

"There is so much to do at Black Butte Ranch that I can't imagine wanting to leave it, with the possible exception of skiing in the winter or going into the town of Sisters, seven miles away. Sisters is a great looking town—just what the ideal Western town should look like."

Hood River Inn

Hood River Village, OR 97031
503-386-2200
Moderate—$45-$65; $6 per extra person, children 10 and under free
AE, CB, DC, MC, V

Directions: From Portland, take I-84 east. Take exit 64. Located ½ mile northeast of junction of Rt 35 and I-84.

At A Glance: Cribs ($4); TV; Outdoor pool; Playground; Pets OK; Babysitting (by pre-arrangement)

This motel is located right on the Columbia River, has lovely views and is set well away from the highway, so it's nice and quiet. The 64 rooms are clean, new, modern, comfortable and roomy, and there is a small reading area on each level with books and magazines. Outdoors there is a large grassy area where kids can play tag or ball, a playground and a heated swimming pool. This is wind surfing territory, and there's a marina down the road where you can rent the equipment to try the sport.

The motel gift shop has limited picnic supplies, wine and food specialties from Hood River. The restaurant attached to the motel has an area for "formal dining" as well as a cafe for lighter, more casual food. You can eat outdoors, overlooking the Columbia River. Service is fast and children are well tolerated. If you want to leave the motel, the dining room at Mt. Hood Lodge is "flexible to crazy requests for food from kids." An outing to Multnomah Falls will turn up both fast food and a dining room with moderate prices.

Comments

"Optimum seasons for visiting are spring, summer and fall. Spring for all the waterfalls and apple blossoms, summer for the good weather, fall for the spectacular leaves and color."

"There is no fence between the grassy area and the river."

20 Teepee
48 hookups

Kah-Nee-Ta Resort

Warm Springs, OR 97761
1-800-831-0100
Inexpensive to Expensive—$20 for teepee; $45-$65 for cottages in Village; $70-$90 for Lodge rooms; mid-week and off-season rates available
AE, CB, DC, MC, V

Directions: From Portland take I-84 to The Dalles. Turn south on Hwy 197, then west on Hwy 216 just before Maupin and travel to Wapinitia. Turn south and head into the reservation.

At A Glance: Cribs; Kitchens; TV; Restaurant; Outdoor pools; Hot mineral baths; Sauna; Horseback riding; Tennis courts; Golf; Bicycle rentals; Hiking trails; Fishing rentals

Kah-Nee-Ta is owned and operated by the Confederated Indian Tribes of Warm Springs. It's the centerpiece of a half-million-acre American Indian reservation, complete with working ranch and wild horses. The resort has two sections—the Lodge and the Village—and an array of accommodations that will fit any budget. At the low, and fun, end of the accommodation scale are authentic teepees, which rent for $20 a night. Bring your sleeping bags, build a fire, and sleep like the Native Americans did. Also in the Village are one- and two-bedroom cottages, some with kitchens. More elaborate quarters on higher ground can be found at the Lodge.

Sun shines over 300 days of the year in Warm Springs, and the warmth of the mineral pools makes swimming a year-round activity. A bigger-than-Olympic-size pool is heated by the hot springs, and hot mineral baths are $3. Miniature golf and biking, white water rafting and trout fishing in the well-stocked Warm Springs River are some of the many things to do on a visit to Kah-Nee-Ta.

The Juniper Room in the Lodge is a very formal dining room with an impressive view. The menu includes buffalo steak and venison, so if your kids like hot dogs and tacos it's probably not a good choice. Make reservations early. The Apaloosa Room serves lunch and breakfast, is informal, and offers the option of eating at poolside. In the Village, the River Room is very informal and well suited to families. Food is tolerable: the best part of the meal is feeding the bread scraps to the hungry and aggressive trout from the deck of the restaurant.

Comments

"Every Saturday night during the summer there is an authentic Indian salmon bake. Sundays at 1 p.m. there is a performance of Indian dancing which the kids really enjoyed. Everyone is encouraged to join in.''

"The only drawback to this resort is the eating, which can be easily resolved by securing a cabin with a kitchen at the Village. Anticipate all your needs in advance as Kah-Nee-Ta is very isolated and the nearest town for supplies or gas is 11 miles away.''

Lake Creek Lodge

Star Route, Sisters, OR 97759
503-595-6331
Expensive—Summer rates are modified American Plan (includes dinner): $80 for 2 in a cottage, $95 for 2 in a house, $170 for 4; each extra person is $35, preschoolers $25; children under 2 free; off-season rates available
No credit cards

Directions: From Portland, take U.S. 26 over Mt. Hood and south on U.S. 97 to Redmond. Take Hwy 126 west to Sisters.

At A Glance: Kitchens; Restaurant; Outdoor pool; Horseback riding; Tennis courts; Hiking trails; Playground; Babysitting (by pre-arrangement)

It's hard to get reservations in July and August at Lake Creek Lodge, since returning guests have first choice, and some families have been coming for 20 years. This is a quaint place, with pine cottages and houses in a wooded setting. Each cottage has a refrigerator and two bedrooms joined by a bathroom; each house has a full kitchen and a living room, some with fireplaces. Beds are comfortable, but there is little sound-proofing between the rooms. There is a lodge with shuffleboard, ping pong, pool table and lots of magazines.

Outdoors, kids 12 and under can fish in the stocked trout stream—be sure to bring your own poles. The heated outdoor pool and two tennis courts are supplemented by a sport court and lawn games like horseshoes.

Breakfast and dinner are served at the Lodge, but not lunch. Food is plain family fare and served buffet style. Children go first and are seated with other kids; adults can bring their own wine. A few high chairs are available.

Comments

"A great place to spend your vacation. I read a 1500-page book by the pool, my husband climbed mountains, the six-year-old fished, rode horses and swam. The baby napped and wandered about in a backpack and had an occasional swim."

"This place is lazy, lovely, relaxed. Kids are not only welcome but catered to."

"Just exploring the woods was absolute heaven for two little boys."

Sunriver Lodge and Resort

Sunriver, OR 97707
1-800-547-3922 or 503-393-1246
Expensive—$70-$90
AE, CB, DC, MC, V

Directions: From Bend, take U.S. 97 South 15 miles.

At A Glance: Cribs; Kitchens; TV; Restaurant; Outdoor pools (2); Sauna; Hot tub; Horseback riding; Tennis courts; Bicycle rentals; Golf; Hiking trails; Ski trails; Fishing rentals; Boat rentals; Playground; Babysitting (by pre-arrangement); Organized activities for kids

Sunriver is a huge (over 3000 acres) resort and residential community designed for those who like wilderness *and* comfort. The natural environment has not been sacrificed and the accommodations are anything but primitive. There are a total of 360 units, including houses, housekeeping suites, and two- and three-bedroom units.

The scenery on this pine and sagebrush studded plateau is spectacular and there is no shortage of activities for all ages. In fact, making a decision as to what to do can be exhausting. There are two 18-hole golf courses, two enormous outdoor pools (plus a diving pool and wading pool), 18 tennis courts (three indoor), stables, marina, bicycle paths, an arts and crafts center, a nature center (complete with a staff naturalist) and heated spas (extra charge). For winter skiing, there are cross-country trails on the resort grounds, and Mt. Bachelor is just 18 miles away for downhill. Of particular interest for families is a great playground complete with forts and a day-care/playroom facility.

In addition to two dining rooms and a coffee shop in the main lodge, there are a number of restaurants (Mexican, Italian, etc.) scattered throughout the resort grounds.

Comments

"We unfortunately chose the most formal of the lodge eateries—The Meadows Dining Room—in which to have our one restaurant meal. The staff tolerated us but the place didn't have that good old family ambience. There's little of interest for young children unless they are precocious enough to enjoy a superb sunset."

"Because the resort is strung out and most people cook in the condos, one might be a little isolated. Unlike other vacations, we didn't meet any other families—and that might be perfect for some people."

"Any hedonist would like Sunriver!"

Timberline Lodge

Timberline Lodge

Timberline, OR 97028
1-800-547-1406; in Oregon 1-800-452-1335; in Portland 503-226-7979
Moderate to Expensive—$48-$95; $8 per extra person
AE, MC, V

Directions: From Portland, take I-84 east. Take Wood Village Exit right to 238th. Follow to Burnside and go left to U.S. 26. Follow signs to lodge.

At A Glance: Cribs; TV; Restaurant; Outdoor pool; Sauna; Hiking trails; Skiing; Babysitting (by pre-arrangement); Organized activities for kids (skiing)

Timberline Lodge is one of the great mountain lodges in the west and is long on stone fireplaces, heavy timbers and large windows with small panes. This beautiful building was built by the WPA and is a national historic landmark. It's a real showplace of arts and crafts, including handmade furniture, fabrics, hand-hooked rugs, mosaics and paintings. The location, 6000 feet up the side of Mt. Hood, makes the surroundings breathtaking on a clear day. Be sure to bring chains for your drive up to the lodge.

Although a number of the rooms are being restored to the original style, many are "up to date" and not particularly attractive. Walls are thin, and accommodations tend to be small.

Skiing is offered year-round at Timberline, and the lifts are right outside the door. You can rent all your gear here. There are lessons for all age levels; the Skiwee program for kids ages 3-12 is a fully supervised program offered seven days a week for full ($38) or half ($28) day. The outdoor pool is kept at 86° and is open all year, so you can swim while it snows.

The dining room at the lodge is long on flair and showmanship and short on quality. They will split portions for kids and have booster seats. It might be better to try the Wy'East Day Lodge, where food is cheaper and served cafeteria style.

Comments

"Desserts on a table at the entrance to the dining room drove some younger kids into a lather."

"Timberline is not a great place for kids under three. They get too cold in the snow, there is no lifeguard at the pool, and once inside, there's little to do save a little ping pong."

Rippling River Resort

68010 E. Fairway Ave., Welches, OR 97067
1-800-547-8054; In Oregon 1-800-452-4612
Moderate to Expensive—$56-$84 for rooms; $120-$140 for condos and
townhouses for 4 people; kids under 18 free; various package deals
AE, CB, DC, MC, V

Directions: From Portland, take I-84 east. Take Wood Village Exit right to 238th. Follow to Burnside and go left to U.S. 26. Follow to Wemme, turn right to Welches Rd. and continue for one mile to the resort. One-hour drive from Portland.

At A Glance: Cribs; Kitchens; TV; Restaurant; Indoor pool; Outdoor pool; Sauna; Hot tubs; Tennis courts; Bicycle rentals; Golf; Babysitting (by pre-arrangement); Organized activities for kids (summer only)

This resort is located on 400 acres on the western slopes of Mt. Hood and consists of 250 units—motel rooms and one-, two- or three-bedroom condominiums and townhouses. Older sections of the facility are very nicely maintained; new sections have modern, northwest architecture. Grounds are spacious, the countryside is wooded, and the feeling is one of quiet and relaxation. Outdoors, activities center around the golf course (27 holes) and swimming pools. There are bike trails, a five-mile jogging path, and six tennis courts. Ample opportunities for activities such as white water rafting or fly fishing on the Salmon River, horseback riding, and skiing at Mt. Hood exist close by the resort. Indoors, a large recreation building houses a big pool with a two-foot wading pool alongside, as well as saunas, hot tub and a game room.

Condominiums and townhouses have kitchens, but if you don't want to cook every meal there are a dining room and a more relaxed coffee shop, which includes an outdoor eating area, at the resort. Both eating spots have high chairs.

Comments
"It's a country club atmosphere in a beautiful part of Oregon."

Quick Reference Index

BOATING AND FISHING

Alderwood Inn
Beach Haven Resort
Black Butte Ranch
Desert Motor Inn
Diablo Lake Resort
Ecologic Place
Elkins Resort
Fort Worden
Green Acres Resort Motel
Harrison Hot Springs
Hidden Valley Ranch
Hill's Resort
Inn at Wapato Point
Islander Lopez
Kah-Nee-Ta
Kelly's Resort
Lake Crescent Lodge
Lake Quinault Lodge
North Beach Inn
North Cascades Lodge
Oak Bay Beach Hotel
Resort at Port Ludlow
Rosario Resort
Sun Mountain Lodge
Sunriver

PLAYGROUND

Alderwood Inn
Beachwood Resort
Desert Motor Inn
Green Acres Resort Motel
Harrison Hot Springs
Holidome
Hood River Inn
Inn at Wapato Point
Islander Lopez

Kelly's Resort
Lake Creek Lodge
Lake Quinault Lodge
North Cascades Base Camp
Orchard Bed and Breakfast
Resort at Port Ludlow
Rosario Resort
Sandpiper Beach Resort
Sunriver

ORGANIZED ACTIVITIES FOR CHILDREN

Black Butte Ranch
Harrison Hot Springs
Rippling River (summer only)
Sun Mountain Lodge
Sunriver
Timberline Lodge (skiing)

PETS OK

Diablo Lake Resort
Edgewater Cottages ($2)
Gateway Inn
Hammett's Mountain Cabin
Harrison Hot Springs
    (bungalows only)
Hill's Resort
Holidome
Idle-A-While Motel
Iron Springs Resort
Kalaloch Lodge
Kelly's Resort
Lake Crescent Lodge
Lake Quinault Lodge (Lakeside
    Inn only, $5)
Last Resort (advance approval)

Mutiny Bay Resort (off-season
   only)
North Beach Inn
Sandpiper Resort ($5)
Sou'wester Lodge
Sun Mountain Lodge

HORSEBACK RIDING

Black Butte Ranch
Green Acres Resort Motel
Hidden Valley Ranch
Kah-Nee-Ta
Lake Creek Lodge
North Cascades Lodge
Sun Mountain Lodge
Sunriver

SKIING

Elkins Resort*
Harrison Hot Springs*
Hidden Valley Ranch*
Hill's Resort*
Idle-A-While Motel*
North Cascades Base Camp
North Cascades Lodge*
Paradise Inn*
Sun Mountain Lodge*
Sunriver*
Timberline Lodge
Village Inn
The Virginian*
Whistler Village Inn

Cross-country skiing

TENNIS

Alderbrook Inn
Black Butte Ranch
Fort Worden
Green Acres Resort Motel
Harrison Hot Springs
Hill's Resort
Idle-A-While Motel
Jacob's Landing
Kah-Nee-Ta
Lake Creek Lodge
Resort at Port Ludlow
Rippling River
Rosario Resort
Sun Mountain Lodge
Sunriver

GOLF

Alderbrook Inn
Black Butte Ranch
Green Acres Resort Motel
Harrison Hot Springs
Jacob's Landing
Kah-Nee-Ta
Resort at Port Ludlow
Rippling River
Sun Mountain Lodge
Sunriver

BICYCLE RENTALS

Black Butte Ranch
Harrison Hot Springs
Inn at Wapato Point
Jacob's Landing
Kah-Nee-Ta

North Cascades Lodge
Orchard Bed and Breakfast
(free)
Resort at Port Ludlow
Rippling River
Sunriver

BEACHCOMBING

Beach Haven Resort
Beachwood Resort
Driftwood Shores
Edgewater Cottages
Fort Worden
Iron Springs Resort
Islander Lopez
Kalaloch Lodge
Klipsan Beach Cottages
Last Resort
Mutiny Bay Resort
North Beach Inn
Rosario Resort
Sandpiper Resort
Sea Sprite
Sou'wester Lodge
Surfsand
Surfview

Green Acres Resort Motel
Harrison Hot Springs**
Hidden Valley Ranch
Holidome*
Hood River Inn
Inn at Wapato Point*
Iron Springs Resort*
Islander Lopez (seasonal)
Jacob's Landing*
Kah-Nee-Ta
Lake Creek Lodge
Lake Quinault Lodge*
Last Resort (seasonal)
Resort at Port Ludlow*
Rippling River**
Rosario Resort**
Royal Scot Motor Inn*
Sun Mountain Lodge
Sunriver
Surfsand*
Surfview*
Timberline Lodge
Village Inn
The Virginian (seasonal)
Whistler Village Inn

*Indoor pool
**Both indoor and outdoor pools

SWIMMING POOL

Alderwood Inn*
Beachwood Resort (seasonal)*
Black Butte Ranch
Blue Horizon Inn*
Campbell's Lodge
Denman Hotel*
Desert Motor Inn
Driftwood Shores*

Index

A

B

C

D

E

Elkins Resort, 105
Ellensburg, 75-76,81
Empress Hotel, 12

F

Florence, 113
Fort Canby State Park, 57
Fort Casey, 37
Fort Columbia, 57
Fort Worden State Park, 46

G

Gastown, 6
Gateway Inn, 68
Georgia-Pacific Corporation, 27
Gingko Petrified Forest, 103-104
Grand Coulee Dam, 104
Green Acres, 18
The Greenbriar Apartments, 9
Grouse Mountain Skyride, 5
Growly Bear Family Bakery, 68

H

Hammett's Mountain Cabin, 85
Harbor Hut, 64
Harrison Hot Springs, 19-20
Haystack Rock, 115
Hidden Valley Ranch, 79
Hill's Resort, 106-107
Hoh Rain Forest, 48
Hoh River, 48
Holidome (Holiday Inn), 81
The Honey Bear Bakery, 87
Hood Canal, 42-44
Hood River Inn, 123
Hurricane Ridge, 47

I

ITT Rayonier Mill Tours, 46
Idaho, North, 103
Idle-a-While Motel, 94
Ilwaco, 57,64
Indian Henri's Wagon Rides, 67
Iron Springs Resort, 61
Island County Fair, 37
The Islander Lopez, 36

J

Jacob's Landing, 28
James Bay Teahouse, 16
Jetfoil, 13

K

Kah-Nee-Ta Resort, 124-125
Kalaloch, 55-56
Kalaloch Lodge, 59
Kelly's Resort, 88
Kelso, 115
Kitsap Peninsula, 42-45
Klipsan Beach Cottages, 63

L

La Famiglia Ristorante, 34
Lady of the Lake, 85,86
Lake Chelan, 82-89
Lake Creek Lodge, 126
Lake Crescent Lodge, 51
Lake Ozette, 55
Lake Quinault Lodge, 52-53
Langley, 37,40
The Last Resort, 45
Lava Butte Geological Area, 120
Leavenworth, 75-78
Ledbetter Point State Park, 57
The Lemon Tree, 116

GOING PLACES

Traveler's Notes

We are interested in your comments on using this travel guide. Did you discover someplace new? Did you have a terrific experience at one of the getaways we listed? Or a disaster? Also tell us about interesting side trips or restaurants you discovered on your travels. If you're the first to recommend a getaway we list in the next edition, we'll send you a complimentary copy of the next *Going Places*.

Name & address of lodging _____

_____

_____

Date of visit _____ *Length of stay* _____

Comments

_____

Your Name _____

Address _____

Phone (_____) _____

Seattle's Child Publishing, P.O. Box 22578, Seattle, WA 98122

GOING PLACES

Traveler's Notes

We are interested in your comments on using this travel guide. Did you discover someplace new? Did you have a terrific experience at one of the getaways we listed? Or a disaster? Also tell us about interesting side trips or restaurants you discovered on your travels. If you're the first to recommend a getaway we list in the next edition, we'll send you a complimentary copy of the next *Going Places*.

Name & address of lodging _____

_____

_____

Date of visit _____ *Length of stay* _____

Comments

_____

Your Name _____

Address _____

Phone (_____) _____

Seattle's Child Publishing, P.O. Box 22578, Seattle, WA 98122

ORDER FORM

Please send me _____ additional copies of GOING PLACES: Family Getaways in the Pacific Northwest. I enclose $7.95 (postage and handling included—Wash. State res. add $.63 tax) for each copy ordered.

Name _____

Address _____

City/State/Zip _____

Phone (_____) _____

Send as a gift to: (Use extra paper for additional gifts.)

Name _____

Address _____

City/State/Zip _____

Gift card should read: _____

Name _____

Address _____

City/State/Zip _____

Gift card should read: _____

Seattle's Child Publishing, P.O. Box 22578, Seattle, WA

From the folks who produced the book!

Seattle's Child—A monthly guide for parents

Seattle's Child is a monthly newspaper for parents, educators, child-care providers and others who care about children. It is a unique resource for the people of the Greater Seattle area, providing information on what to do and where to go with children.

Features include a monthly calendar of events for children, ideas for outings and reviews of current plays, movies, books and restaurants appropriate for families. There are feature articles on a wide range of issues that affect children and those who care for them.

In addition, annual supplements broaden the scope and usefulness of **Seattle's Child** — *Summer Learning* provides a listing of summer camps and classes for children 12 and under. The *Education Directory* , published in the early spring, lists educational options and opportunities for Seattle area children.

Subscribe now!
One year/$12 or Two years/$18

How to subscribe:

Call (206)322-2594 or return this coupon:

☐ *1 year/$12* ☐ *2 years/$18*   ☐ *New* ☐ *Renew (extend)*

Name _____

*Address*_____

City/State/Zip _____

Phone Number (_____)_____

　　　☐ *Bill me*

　　　☐ *Check enclosed for $_____*

　　　☐ *Visa* ☐ *Mastercard*

　　　Card#_____ Exp. date_____

Mail to: Seattle's Child , P.O. Box 22578, Seattle, WA 98122